Cecil G. Osborne

PRAYER AND YOU

Word Books, Publisher
Waco, Texas

PRAYER AND YOU

Library of Congress catalog card number: 74-78043
Printed in the United States of America

Scripture quotations, unless otherwise noted, are from The Revised Standard Version of the Bible, copyrighted 1946 (renewed 1973), 1956 and © 1971 by the Division of Christian Education of the National Council of the Churches of Christ in the U.S.A., and are used by permission.

Quotations from *The New English Bible* (NEB), © The Delegates of The Oxford University Press and The Syndics of The Cambridge University Press, 1961, 1970, are used by permission.

The quotation marked TEV is from *Good News For Modern Man*, Today's English Version of the New Testament, copyright © American Bible Society 1966, and is used by permission.

The quotation marked Phillips is from J. B. Phillips, *The New Testament in Modern English* (revised edition), copyright © 1958, 1960, 1972 by J. B. Phillips and published by The Macmillan Company.

Quotations marked KJV are from the Authorized or King James Version of the Bible.

The quotation from Andrew Weil, *The Natural Mind: A New Way of Looking at Drugs and the Higher Consciousness,* is used by permission of the publisher, Houghton Mifflin.

Contents

Introduction

"EVERYONE HAS a problem, is a problem, or lives with a problem," Sam Shoemaker once said in a sermon. I believe that. The very fact of our existence in this complex world poses a problem. There may be no particular crisis facing you at the moment, but you are probably not as happy or fulfilled as God meant you to be. Some of your relationships are perhaps not all they might be.

The creative kind of relationship with the Eternal which we call prayer can open up new channels for growth and fulfillment. This book deals, in part, with the way in which a minister blundered toward the light, making innumerable mistakes along the way, and finally emerged with a much clearer picture of what prayer is all about. It is possible that you may identify with me, and gain some glimmer of truth from my own search.

Although I am chronologically eligible for the Geritol Club, and rejoice that Social Security set in before rigor mortis, I feel in some ways that I am just becoming fit to live. I never enjoyed life more. I am busier than I have ever been in my life, and probably more effective, which is the way it should be. Most of these dividends I attribute to some insights concerning prayer and life—some of which I have dealt with in this book.

In part this is an account of my earlier misconceptions about prayer. A few of them were devastating when I mistook my earnest desires for the will of God. It also deals with

7

my discovery that one big part of prayer is, in essence, the sum total of one's reaction to all of life, verbalized or simply felt at the center of one's being.

Thousands must have discovered it long before I did, but gradually it dawned upon me that prayer is not what we *say*, but what we *feel*. For instance if, from some vague sense of duty, I pray, "Lord, bless Mary and John, who are having marital difficulties," but feel relatively indifferent, my actual prayer is, "Lord, I don't really care very much *what* happens to Mary and John." The spoken prayer must be in harmony with the inner feeling, or it is largely a waste of time.

If I pray fervently for physical health, but unconsciously desire illness so that I can be dependent, or receive attention (a substitute for love), I will get sickness, not health. It will not matter how earnestly I verbalize my need for health if my unconscious need to be cared for is greater. The Psalmist must have had this in mind when he prayed, "Clear thou me from hidden faults." [1] That is, "Lord, reveal to me what it is that I may be hiding from myself, so that I can be totally honest with you."

The word "prayer" automatically takes on for most of us the connotation of supplication—of asking for something—but there are many other forms: gratitude, intercessory prayer, adoration, a silent yearning of the soul, a cry of grief or anger when we have lost something or someone we hold dear. In fact, conversation with God—which is one important aspect of prayer—can take on as many forms as a conversation with any human being, and should be just as natural.

How your relationship with your human father affects your feelings about God; how anger can be as valid a part of prayer as adoration; how your metabolism or emotional state can affect your praying; why some people should always pray to Jesus instead of to God—these and the account of some of my own trials and errors—and victories—are dealt with in this book. I breathe a silent prayer at this moment, hoping that you may find somewhere in it a ray of hope and a glimmer of truth from a fellow searcher.

I.
Success and Failure
in Prayer

I FIND IT VERY GRATIFYING that the Apostle Paul and I have at least one thing in common. We both had some unanswered prayers. He says that he prayed three times for an unnamed thorn in the flesh to be removed. He received an answer ("My grace is sufficient for you"),[1] but this was not precisely what he had initially hoped for.

Many years ago I prayed very earnestly about something, with devastating results. I had made a little money in some fortunate investments, and an opportunity arose to invest in an enterprise which looked very promising. Three or four of my friends were interested in the venture. We pooled our resources, but lacked a few thousand dollars of having enough to complete the deal.

I prayed about it, and used a time-honored, if dubious, method. I said, "Lord, if the additional funds become available to me, I will go into this venture. If not, I will take it to mean that I am not to do so." Almost miraculously, it seemed, I received the precise amount of money shortly thereafter, and we went ahead with the project.

Well, almost from the outset the project was a fiasco. One of the leading participants, who was to manage the enterprise, proved to be hopelessly inept. Not only was the manager a bungler, he was just slightly dishonest. You can

11

protect yourself from an obvious crook. An honest man you can deal with openly. But someone who is honest just part of the time is more difficult to cope with. The entire thing was a disaster. It was not merely the financial loss but the incredible amount of time it consumed untangling the mess that made the enterprise so unfortunate.

Prayer and Intense Desire

So, I had prayed, named a condition which had been met, and the project was a disaster. Apparently, there was something seriously wrong with this old principle of "open and closed doors." It was an expensive lesson. If, instead of invoking some magic formula, I had used my God-given intelligence and checked with more knowledgeable people in the field, I might have avoided the mistake.

Actually, my intense desire to invest in that particular venture constituted the *real* prayer, which was, "Lord, I am determined to make this investment." I doubt if I would have been deterred even if the additional funds had not become available. What I wanted at the center of my being was the real prayer. The *words* of my prayer were not in harmony with my intense inner desire. My attitude was something akin to that of an elderly woman who complained to the Better Business Bureau about a fraud that had been perpetrated upon her. Asked why she hadn't checked with the Bureau before making the investment, she replied, "I was afraid you'd tell me not to do it."

I once had a summer home on a beautiful lake in Northern Michigan. One morning I took two young sons of a neighbor fishing. The lake was nine miles long and about four miles wide. The best fishing spot was roughly two miles from my dock. I had an ancient but fairly reliable outboard motor, and in a few minutes we were happily fishing. After an hour or so I noticed a cloud gathering in the distance, but the fishing was good, and I was oblivious to the fact that the cloud had been getting darker and closer.

Soon it began to sprinkle, and I remembered that a few

weeks before two men had drowned while fishing in the lake when a sudden storm had struck. I pulled up anchor and we started for shore.

Then it hit. It was the most ferocious storm I had ever experienced. With the rain there came a violent wind from off shore. Waves threatened to swamp the boat, as I frantically kept trying to head it into them. To have gotten into a trough would have been disastrous. The wind intensified, and the driving rain was so violent that I could not see beyond the bow of the boat and had to shield my eyes from its blinding force. Having swung the bow of the boat this way and that a hundred times to keep heading into the waves, I eventually lost all sense of direction.

The spark plugs on the ancient outboard motor were exposed, and near-panic set in as I wondered how long it would be before they would be shorted out in that downpour. I wondered, too, whether I was headed toward the other end of the lake—at least six or eight miles away—toward my own dock, or going in circles.

In this predicament I prayed, but I did *not* say, "O Thou most gracious deity, who dwellest in the farthest reaches of space as well as in the human heart, I, though sinful and unworthy, beseech Thy tender mercies in my hour of need. I pray that as Jesus stilled the waves, so may this storm abate and the winds subside."

No, my prayer was almost identical with that of Simon Peter who, after a few impetuous steps on the water, began to sink. He cried out, "Lord, save me!" [2] My brief prayer, like his, was succinct, heartfelt, and to the point. Every nerve ending in my body was praying.

After what seemed an interminable time, during which the aged motor kept on roaring, suddenly the wind abated and the rain turned into a steady drizzle. I looked up to see my dock not five feet in front of me! Gratitude is no word for what I felt. I didn't even have to thank God. Every part of my being that had been seeking the guidance of God now thanked him.

The next morning the sun was shining, and it seemed like a good day for fishing. Before starting out I removed the gas tank cap and put a stick down to see how much gasoline was left. The stick came up dry! There was not enough gas in the tank to wet the end of the stick. I sank weakly onto the dock and for a long time I stared at that boat, its decrepit motor, and the empty tank. Suddenly I realized that I had not cut off the motor at the dock. It had just run out of gas at the last moment and coasted the last few yards. I sat and felt great waves of gratitude. Words were inadequate.

Visualization in Prayer

There is another aspect of prayer which I have come to feel is very important. I had had a serious sore throat for some weeks. Penicillin and antibiotics had no effect on it. Looking back on the experience I can see how an impaired relationship and its accompanying emotional stress had precipitated the whole thing, but it was not obvious to me at the time.

Finally my throat got somewhat better about a week before my wife, my son, and I left for a trip through Europe and the Middle East. In London the sore throat became worse and I looked up a physician.

"Ah, yes; we'll fix that up in no time," he said as he reached for a bottle and a swab. I said, "Hold it. Whenever my throat is swabbed out it gets worse. Try something else." He smiled indulgently and painted my throat with creosote, or something which felt and smelled like it. The next morning I was worse. In Rome I went to a clinic, and they tried the same procedure. "Yes, very red and raw," the doctor said. "Very simple." Over my protest he swabbed it with what felt like sulphuric acid. The next day I could barely swallow.

It was not a strep infection, but something which yielded to no form of treatment. In four or five cities I went to clinics or hospitals. It became steadily worse.

In Lucerne one morning I urged my wife and son to go out

and see the Jungfrau, which I had visited a year or two before. I would stay in bed to see if rest would do my throat
any good. Resting in bed I decided to look through my pocket
New Testament searching for something I could focus on.
My eye finally fell on the words of Jesus, "According to your
faith be it unto you." [3] I had been praying for God to do
something about my throat, and here was Jesus telling me it
was all up to me.

So, it's according to my faith, I said. *It's all up to me to
tap the divine healing forces surrounding me.* I'd known
that for years. I even had a couple of good sermons on the
theme. But how could I summon faith I didn't feel? All I
could feel was an excruciating pain every time I swallowed.

All right, I said, *I am going to visualize my throat as
being well. God does not will sickness or any other malfunction. He wills wholeness of mind, body and spirit. If I am
sick or in pain, it is because in some way I am out of harmony.*

I spent the next few hours in bed reading, meditating,
trying to get my emotions in harmony with the universal,
beneficent, cosmic laws which surround us. Then I decided
to "see" myself as well, healed, able to swallow without pain.

Can I visualize myself as being without pain by tonight?
No.

*Can I visualize rising in the morning able to swallow
without pain?* No.

How about noon tomorrow? The feeling was negative.

By tomorrow night? No.

How about the second morning? Yes! For some reason I
do not understand I could visualize a sudden, total healing of
my throat by the second morning.

All during the day, whenever I swallowed—which must
have been a thousand times—I visualized myself getting out
of bed the second morning without a sore throat. I had
plenty of motivation, because the very act of swallowing re-
minded me to see complete healing on my mental screen.

A secret doubt crept in. Maybe just remaining in bed all

day would do the trick. Perhaps it was just rest I needed. But that night, despite a day of complete rest, my throat was worse. The next morning it was much worse. I went out the following day, trying to avoid swallowing and to forget the pain that was there even when I didn't swallow. That night it was no better, but I still kept seeing myself getting out of bed the next morning with no sore throat.

That second morning I was up, shaving, when suddenly it dawned on me. No sore throat! Not the slightest trace. It never came back. I don't explain it. I can only report what happened.

Violating a Biblical Principle

A disappointing sequel should be reported. Several years later I came down with another sore throat during a busy week. I tried the same procedure again, only this time I cheated a little. My schedule was so hectic I felt that I simply couldn't take off a full day. So I stayed in bed until about eleven, and went to my office resolved to keep the healing thought in my mind all during the day. It didn't work. My attention was diverted in a hundred ways. I was violating the biblical principle, "You will seek me and find me; when you seek me with all your heart." [4] That means, as I see it, that the whole organism must be focused upon God. The first time all of my psychic energy had been focused upon God's power and love and goodness. The second time my energies and attention were diffused, and nothing happened.

Many people have a feeling that if only they can be virtuous enough, their prayers will be answered; but if they are not "good," they dare not pray with any deep expectation. There is an element of truth in this. "If our hearts do not condemn us, we have confidence before God; and we receive from him whatever we ask, because we keep his commandments and do what pleases him." [5] In other words, if we feel unworthy, or out of harmony with God, our faith is weakened. But the limitation is all on our part, not on his. We are loved not because we are *good*, but because we are *his*. The outwardly virtuous Pharisees received nothing from Jesus, whereas the moral derelicts, the ones whom the Pharisees termed "sinners," were being healed by the hundreds. Nothing good or virtuous you do causes him to love you more; and nothing evil you do causes him to love you less. It is not his love that is diminished by our human defects, but our faith.

Turning Loose

There is a natural, almost universal, tendency to think of sin as some overt act. Jesus makes it clear, however, that the more serious of the sins are spiritual: pride, greed, envy, lust, materialism, lack of compassion, arrogance.[6] One of my own spiritual sins of which I become aware again and again is an insidious sense of self-sufficiency, first cousin to pride. Its origin was innocent enough: the awareness that I was on my own. I learned that I could do whatever I had to do to survive. To a point this can be a virtue. Any virtue, however, carried to an extreme can become a vice.

Chiefly through the generosity and interest of a man who headed a foundation, a considerable amount of money was made available to me to explore the use of small groups as a spiritual growth device. The grant lasted three years, and during that time we experimented, explored, innovated, and adapted various methods in an effort to find ways of stimulating emotional and spiritual growth through small groups. Our experimental groups were held in homes, churches, and in prisons. Several thousand people participated. We discovered a means of keeping small spiritual growth groups alive and vital. Later we linked up our work with the national Yokefellow movement, and our materials and methods spread into all fifty states and many foreign countries.

A year before the money was exhausted I began a search for additional funds. I worked at it diligently for six months, but every door was closed. I used all of the ingenuity I could muster, without any positive results.

Finally one morning, in a half-hour quiet time I said, "Lord, I think you want this work continued. Maybe you don't. If not, then I don't either. It would be a mess if I tried on my own to continue something that should stop right now. I am willing to have it end or continue. I will leave it up to you. I'll stop trying to find ways of financing it. I give it all over to you. I will do anything I am led to do, but right now I don't know where to turn."

Nothing wonderful happened immediately. But every morning in my quiet time I reaffirmed my prayer, and searched my soul for some subtle, unconscious reluctance to let God have his way. One morning I wanted nothing—a difficult feat for me. Then slowly, on a little projection screen I keep in the front of my mind there appeared the words, "All things are yours," [7] a quotation from one of Paul's letters. *Yes, I know that. Fine. Is that all?*

Then a second line appeared on the screen. "Receive it then." *Fine. But how? When?* In a moment a third line appeared on the bottom of the screen, "It's all taken care of." *Great!* Now I could drop the problem and relinquish it completely. I put it out of my mind, secure in the knowledge that the answer was on the way.

Relinquishment does not mean giving up, or abandoning something, but turning it over to the Father. So I let him take over. In my stubborn, egocentric pride I had been trying to do it alone. Now I turned it loose.

One morning months later, as I sat at my desk thinking of something else, a sudden thought came. "Why don't you call Bill?" I knew it had to do with the problem I had relinquished. I phoned him in Los Angeles, four hundred miles away. "Bill," I said, "I have an idea. I have proposed it to a dozen other people and they think I'm crazy. I want to talk to you about it."

"Fly down today," he replied, "and I'll meet you at the airport." A sixty-minute flight put me at the Los Angeles airport. We had a cup of coffee, and in fifteen minutes had worked out a plan which enabled the West Coast Yokefellow Center to become a permanently self-supporting reality. It had started with a foundation grant, one secretary and a desk in a tiny office. It became a self-sustaining operation with a staff of twelve, and no need to solicit funds. In the next few years over sixty thousand people were involved in small groups, using ideas and materials we developed during the first three years.

I do not see this as particularly earth-shaking; but I have heard from thousands of people whose lives have been changed as a result. To me this is gratifying evidence that when I abandon my self-sufficiency and tune into the limitless resources of God, significant things happen. I am firmly convinced that if I could believe that at a still deeper level, much more good could be accomplished, since he "is able to do far more abundantly than all that we ask or think." [8]

What Prayer Is Not

Prayer does not involve magic, or the miraculous, despite verifiable reports of instantaneous physical healing, or seemingly inexplicable answers to prayer. Prayer does not violate or alter natural physical laws. Some answers to prayer which seem beyond explanation are apparently the result of a higher law having superseded a lower one. For instance, the law of gravity causes steel to sink in water, but a vast ocean liner, made of millions of pounds of steel, will float. A higher law has superseded the law of gravity.

Prayer is not primarily a means of "making life easier." After Jesus had fed the five thousand with five loaves and two small fish, the mob surged after him shouting, "Lord, give us this bread always"! [9] They tried to make him king on a platform of "Bread without work."

Prayer is not intended to be a means of changing other people so that life will be easier for us. Two women "prayer partners" prayed daily that the husband of one of the women would stop drinking. It was a seemingly legitimate subject for prayer. After some weeks the husband suddenly announced that he was through with alcohol forever, and he stopped drinking completely. He stopped, that is, until one day his wife said quite sharply, "That's the third time I've told you to take out the garbage!" He promptly went out and got drunk, and continued to drink despite a stepped-up program of prayer on the part of the two women. At no time did the wife ask in prayer if she might be contributing to the problem.

The relating of remarkable instances of answered prayer can make it seem as though these were everyday events. Frankly, they are not, at least in the lives of most Christians I have known. Would that they were! But they aren't. The most that we can hope for is that our oneness with the Father, and growth in his love, can increase the frequency of the times our prayers are the kind which God can grant. Some have discovered that their most gratifying periods of prayer are when they are in silent, wordless, loving communion with God, wanting nothing, asking nothing, but simply enjoying his presence. This fulfills the promise: "Take delight in the Lord, and he will give you the desires of your heart." [10]

2.
Your Faith Can Make You Whole —or Sick

IT IS NOT DIRECTLY stated that Job had been brooding over the possibility that he might be overwhelmed by a succession of calamities. But Job himself seems to suggest that possibility when he says that the disastrous things he had so greatly feared had come upon him. Does negative thinking set up negative vibrations, or a "force field," which make us more susceptible to destructive events? Does a positive, believing, and affirmative attitude set cosmic forces in motion which tend to bring desirable and creative things into our lives? There is much evidence that this is so. Carl Jung believed this to be true.

I have seen people with positive attitudes toward life receive a disproportionate share of "good things," and conversely, I have observed innumerable instances of disastrous results from negative thinking.

A church officer once reported to me that his wife was seriously ill at home. I asked if I might call, but he said that she was very weak and preferred not to have visitors. I inquired if she had seen a doctor. He said, "No, she has cancer. Her sister died of cancer, and my wife has the same symptoms. She feels that it's useless to go to a hospital. She prefers to die at home." His manner indicated that it would be futile to reason with either of them.

21

I assured him that I would pray for her, and asked him to report on her condition. A few weeks later when she could no longer take food and was virtually skin and bones, he carried her to his car and took her to the hospital. X-rays revealed no sign of a tumor, or any other physical problem. Her physician told her there was nothing wrong with her except fear. She went home, and gradually regained her health. "Scared to death" is more than a figure of speech. She had come very close to being frightened to death as the result of a negative belief.

In my office I have a beautiful painting done by my wife. It's a lovely abstract in different tones of yellows and golds. Yellow is the color of hope, expectation, sunrise, newness of life. It's a cheerful, happy painting.

One day I had been counseling a young woman who was deeply depressed. As she paused near the door, close to the picture, I asked her how she liked the painting.

"I don't like it," she said.

"What is it about the picture you dislike?"

She pointed to one very faint dark spot near the bottom, the only one in the picture, and said, "It's such a gloomy picture; all dark and forbidding." In her depression all she could see was the one faint dark area. The radiant yellow tones, bright with promise and hope, had all escaped her. When one is in a state of deep depression, nothing looks right. The whole world is gloomy.

Praying to the Symptom

If you have ulcers or asthma, or other symptoms, and pray earnestly enough and frequently enough about them, they will probably get worse. You are "praying to the symptom." If you pray about an alcoholic husband or wife, or a rebellious child, or any other physical, emotional or circumstantial problem, and focus on the problem, it can get worse. The reason, of course, is that you are focusing on the problem; or rather, on the symptom of the problem. It is really "praying to the problem," reaffirming its reality, instead of focusing on God's love and his power to heal.

A friend of mine suffered from neurodermatitis, a skin ailment which had defied every form of medical treatment for years. She prayed about it, but it got worse as she focused more of her attention on it. In a Yokefellow group she mentioned a violent disagreement with a relative which had been going on over a period of years. Someone asked, "Could there be some connection between your skin problem and your hostility?" She rejected the idea at first, but finally agreed that perhaps she had been praying about the symptom, without dealing with the real source. She resolved the impaired relationship, and within a matter of days her skin condition cleared up, never to return.

A woman whom I knew quite well suffered from an amazing variety of ailments. She spent a month or more out of every year in a hospital. There were stubborn infections which refused to heal, despite all that medical science could do for her. When eventually some medication could be found which would relieve the symptom, she would go home and engage in a period of intense activity. Before long she would be back in the hospital with another ailment. She reacted adversely to almost every form of medication. This went on for years. She could be labeled masochistic, or sickness-prone—which in a sense she was—but these are simply terms used to describe a personality malfunction.

Her father had been masochistic—accident-prone, trouble-prone, and failure-prone. He suffered an almost endless series of unfortunate events. He was a fine Christian who believed all of the proper doctrines, went to church regularly, and abided by all of the standard moral and ethical codes. But he was a hopelessly negative personality. He was suspicious, judgmental, and, of course, unconsciously he hated himself. His sense of inferiority was so great that he found it impossible to see much good in the world, or in people. His entire outlook was negative.

His daughter, who loved, feared, needed, and unconsciously hated him (or at least his dogmatic negativism), never resolved her ambivalent feelings about him. The inner conflict was tearing her apart emotionally and physically. She was a fine, cheerful, unselfish, self-reliant individual; but her endless list of physical ailments, of course, bore a relationship to the emotional battle raging within her.

The Futility of Pursuing Incompatible Goals

Some of her father's negativism showed occasionally through this woman's external cheerfulness. Guilt is essentially trying to pursue incompatible goals. She was determinedly trying to be cheerful and unselfish, but underneath she was still struggling with her father, and that part of him that was in her, genetically and environmentally. Outwardly positive and life-affirming, inwardly she felt inferior, tense, anxious and guilty over the unresolved conflict about her feelings toward her father. She was unable to resolve her conflict, and to the end of her days refused to face the conflicting forces raging within her. Her physical symptoms never cleared up.

Many persons are outwardly cheerful and positive, yet unconsciously have a self-defeating, negative attitude which sets up all manner of conflicting emotional currents. Since none of us sees ourselves clearly, no matter how introspective we are or how honest we try to be, where there are inner conflicts of this type, the help of a skilled, perceptive counselor or therapy group is usually required.

Ten members of a Yokefellow group were sitting around on the floor one evening. The mood was one of relaxed informality. One relatively new member of the group had shared something, and a young woman said very gently and thoughtfully, "Amy, I like you but I don't think I could trust you. I feel you would either try to manipulate me or lie to me, if you thought it would serve your purpose. I would like to be able to trust you, but at the moment I don't. Perhaps it's all in me. Maybe it's my problem entirely. But that's my honest feeling."

We knew Amy's story, which had involved an unbelievably traumatic childhood. In order to survive incredible hardships, she had lied and manipulated people. She had never learned to give or receive love, for she had been too badly hurt to trust love.

Amy looked thoughtful. "Yes," she said, "I think you're right. I do manipulate and scheme to get what I want. But that's not the kind of person I really want to be."

Her honesty was beautiful. When the group ended that evening we stood in a circle, our arms about each other in silence, feeling a sense of love and oneness. I asked, "What do you feel?" Someone said, "Love." Then other responses came:

"Oneness."

"Security."

"Wanted."

"Like I belong."

Then Amy said, "I feel loved." Since she had never known love in her home as a child, or in her marriage, this was a major breakthrough for her. When I saw her the next week she looked different. Some of the haunted, defensive look was gone, and she appeared more relaxed. The love of God, mediated through accepting persons, had already begun to work.

Not having been loved as a child, Amy could not have had a positive attitude toward life until she learned to trust, then love, a small group of people who genuinely cared enough to be honest with her.

He Is Able to Do More Than We Ask

There is a fascinating story in the New Testament in which there was a positive response despite a negative attitude on the part of a praying group of people. Herod had killed James, and since this seemed to please a large number of influential people, he imprisoned Peter. A little band of believers gathered in the home of Mary, the mother of John Mark, and prayed for Peter. The implication is that they knew their prayers would not be instrumental in releasing him, but because they loved him they prayed for him.

During that night, Peter was miraculously released. He went straight to the home where the prayer meeting was being held and knocked on the door. Rhoda, a servant girl, went to the door. When she recognized Peter's voice, she was so happy that she ran back to the group without opening the door, and announced excitedly that Peter was standing outside.

"You're crazy!" they told her. But she insisted that it was true. So they responded, "It's his angel."

"Meanwhile, Peter kept on knocking. They opened the door at last and when they saw him they were amazed." [1]

Their concern for Peter had been genuine, and certainly there were deep desire and intensity in their prayers, though they had not dreamed of praying for his release. But in this instance God—as he so often does—demonstrated again that "he is able to do far more abundantly than all we ask or think." [2]

The power of negative thinking—and praying—was dramatically demonstrated to me in the case of a friend. Despite a high degree of intelligence and considerable ability, he was very suggestible. Unfortunately his family physician was incredibly lacking in tact. An X-ray had been taken, and my friend waited anxiously for the physician to give him the verdict. The doctor looked at it, frowned, and said, "This doesn't look too good. But just to be sure I'll have an associate check it over. We'll give you a final opinion tomorrow."

Convinced that he was doomed, the patient went home and spent a sleepless night. He was sure the doctor was trying to let him down easy. He was told a few days later that the X-ray results revealed that there was nothing wrong. But he "knew the worst." A week later he was admitted to a mental institution. He was there for over a year. My friend was the victim of an excessive amount of suggestibility, and abnormal fear of death (due, I learned later, to an unresolved guilt problem) and a remarkably obtuse physician. His negative "faith" (belief) had made him emotionally ill.

God Wills Our Best

Some time ago, at a retreat I met a terribly depressed woman. She was married to a wealthy man, and lived in a magnificent home which she hated. He had chosen it, which was, of course, a mistake of major magnitude. The marriage was not going well, and she was so depressed that she lacked any interest in life. The thought of entertaining a few people seemed a burden too great to bear. Life had lost all meaning.

Since the glands and the emotions are interrelated, I suspected a hormone imbalance. But we both knew that there was more to her depression than that. In counseling sessions we dealt with all of the factors which contributed to her depression—rejection in the past as well as in the present, the deprecation by her husband, and a dozen other factors.

During the course of the counseling, though she tried to force herself to act normally, I could see that she could just as easily have chosen death as life. She had everything to live on, and nothing to live for. "If I were not a Christian," she said, "I'd take an overdose of pills."

At no point did we ever pray about her depression, of course. That would have been focusing upon the problem; in fact, praying to the problem. But we did dwell upon God's perfect will for her, which involved love, joy, peace, and happiness.

She did need hormone shots, and got them. But her chemical imbalance was in a sense the result of her emotional imbalance. In time, as the result of some intensive therapy, she became a far more radiant person than she had ever been before. She wrote:

"I've never been happier in my life, though my marriage

seems hopeless. I am free at last of the fear that has haunted me all my life. The depression is gone, and my friends are divided into two groups: half of them predict that this is a temporary euphoria which will pass, and the other half openly envy me. The truth is that I have come alive at last. Self-hate and fear are gone. God is very real, and at last I'm *living*."

Negative Thinking Is Just a Bad Habit

Negative thinking and positive thinking are both habits. You can have it either way. The choice is yours. Due to certain early childhood inputs, I have a slight tendency to look first on the dark side, to search for the pitfalls, before evaluating the positive aspects.

My wife and I were going for a walk on the beach one day. We parked the car on a bluff above the sandy beach and walked down a trail to the shore. As we stepped from a flat rock to the sand below, we both noticed something at the same time. A pile of rotting seaweed had attracted an enormous swarm of flies. The seaweed lay on the purest, whitest sand I had ever seen. As we stepped off the rock we both said simultaneously, "Look at the——" but our final words of the sentence were different. My sentence came out: "Look at the nasty swarm of flies." Her exclamation was, "Look at the beautiful white sand!" We both laughed. I saw the flies, she saw the beauty of the sand.

Somewhat lamely I said, "Well, after all, you're an artist and are on the lookout for beauty. I am a realist and must face the grim realities of life." Then we laughed again. "That's the weakest rationalization I ever came up with," I said, "but it's the best I can do at the moment."

If some aspects of your early life (where most of our fundamental tendencies are formed) have made you somewhat negative or critical, you can train yourself to become a positive, affirmative person by practice. Like any other skill or art, it takes time and practice.

You will have to practice it every day of your life. Begin

by thanking God for life. You are alive, and even if life is not all it might be, you are better off than roughly three-fourths of the world's population. Look for things about you during the day for which you can be grateful. Complaining and criticizing are just bad habits, and they can be overcome by practicing the habit of thanking God for the lovely and beautiful aspects of life.

The psalmists were, in general, neither Pollyannas who refused to see the darker side of life, nor depressed, negative pessimists who saw only gloom and despair. They were basically realistic. Many people have puzzled over what are called the imprecatory psalms, those masterpieces of invective in which the psalmist calls down the wrath of God upon his enemies. There is no great mystery here. When the psalmist angrily demands that God punish his enemies, he is simply expressing his honest feelings. There is no pretense. A man of strong passions, David loved and hated with intensity. In the 109th Psalm, for instance, he calls down vengeance upon the head of an enemy:

Appoint a wicked man against him;
    let an accuser bring him to trial.
When he is tried, let him come forth guilty;
    let his prayer be counted as sin!
May his days be few;
    may another seize his goods!
May his children be fatherless,
    and his wife a widow!
May his children wander about and beg;
    may they be driven out of the ruins they inhabit!
May the creditor seize all that he has;
    may strangers plunder the fruits of his toil!
Let there be none to extend kindness to him,
    nor any to pity his fatherless children!
May his posterity be cut off;
    may his name be blotted out in the second generation!
May the iniquity of his fathers be remembered before
        the Lord,
    and let not the sin of his mother be blotted out!
                                                PSALM 109:6–14

These verses seem to be utterly devoid of compassion, and filled, rather, with venom and hatred. Many other psalms are equally vitriolic. However, let it be remembered that this is good therapy. I recommend it.

Let Your Anger Out—Appropriately

When you are feeling outraged over some injustice, sit down and write a letter. Make it a hot one! Express every negative feeling you have. Tell the other person off. Spare no expletive. Make it strong, violent, real. Fill up the pages with all of the anger and violence you feel in your soul. You are surely as human as David, "a man after God's own heart."

But, of course, *don't mail it!* Just write it. If your pen or typewriter can't keep up with the angry explosions, talk it out. Scream it out, making sure the doors are closed and the children or neighbors can't hear. God listens in and understands, just as he understood the indignation of David. Don't be a phony sweet Christian at that moment. Be your human, angry, vengeful self. Let all the repressed anger out. Finally, spent and exhausted, you may come to the place where you can even vent your self-pity, as David so often did.

We love to quote the beautiful 23rd Psalm, but the 22nd is in some ways even more interesting. In it David wallows in self-pity. He tells of all his woes, speaks of his numerous enemies, and complains of all the injustices he has suffered at the hands of his foes. At least he is honest. That is precisely how he felt at the moment. But toward the end, as he exhausts his anger, and his depression is dissipated, he begins to extol the glory of God: "All the ends of the world shall remember and turn to the Lord; and all the families of the nations shall worship before him." [3]

David was probably somewhat of a manic-depressive. He could sink to the lowest depths of depression, then rise to the heights of ecstasy. Poet, warrior, ruler, musician, he felt the whole range of emotions and expressed them in writing.

That's good therapy! I recommend it, in a suitable setting. Along with the legitimate emotions of rage and indignation, let the positive emotions be expressed as well when they are felt. David, in the eighth Psalm, exults:

O Lord, our Lord,
    how majestic is thy name in all the earth!
. . . .
When I look at thy heavens, the work of thy fingers,
    the moon and the stars which thou hast established;
what is man that thou art mindful of him,
    and the son of man that thou dost care for him?
Yet thou hast made him little less than God,
    and dost crown him with glory and honor.
Thou hast given him dominion over the works of thy hands;
    thou hast put all things under his feet,
all sheep and oxen,
    and also the beasts of the field,
the birds of the air, and the fish of the sea,
    whatever passes along the paths of the sea.

O Lord, our Lord,
    how majestic is thy name in all the earth!

PSALM 8

How to Handle Negative Emotions

There are three main ways of handling negative emotions:

Express them—which may or may not be appropriate, depending upon the circumstances.

Suppress them—that is, to be aware of the feelings, but to "sit on them" because it would be inappropriate to express them just then.

Repress them—which is the most dangerous of all. This means to deny to ourselves that we have these feelings. The roots of repression go back to earliest childhood, when many of us were taught never to express negative feelings. This is a lie to the self. If I am angry I am *angry*. If I feel jealous or envious or irritated, it is dishonest to pretend that I do not have these emotions, just because they are "not Christian."

It is far better to be honest, as David was, than to lie to myself and others, and pretend that I do not feel the whole gamut of emotions common to all humanity in some degree.

There is one higher law than the law of honesty. It is the law of love. Honesty may cause me to feel that I ought to tell someone off. Love for that person can cause me to suppress (withhold) the expression. I have no right to crush another person just because I want to be honest.

If negative feelings, or depression, afflict you from time to time, remind yourself again of the varying emotions of the Psalmist:

In Psalm 3:6: "I am not afraid of ten thousands of people who have set themselves against me."

In the very next verse: "Thou dost smite all mine enemies on the cheek, thou dost break the teeth of the wicked."

In the 6th Psalm: "My soul also is sorely troubled. But thou, O Lord—how long? . . . I am weary with my moaning; every night I flood my bed with tears; I drench my couch with my weeping."

But in the 13th Psalm after an initial burst of self-pity, he writes, "I will sing to the Lord, because he has dealt bountifully with me."

If your spiritual and emotional life has its ups and downs, you may take some consolation from the fact that the heroes of the Bible, from Job to St. Paul, all had the same problem. This is a part of our humanity. The important thing is to remember that if there is a dark night of the soul, there is also a sunrise. To live in the shadows is very depressing, but you are the only one who can make the decision to walk out into the sunshine and thank God for the sun, for life, for beauty, for hope.

Negative Thinking Holds Onto the Past

Occasional bouts of depression are normal. Periodic depression is fatal only if you let negative thinking become a permanent attitude of life.

At a retreat for married couples which I conducted, one

of the men told me, "We brought an estranged couple with us who are separated. My wife and I had been praying that they would come, and they're here." During the week neither expressed a desire for a personal conference. I breathed a prayer for guidance.

Just before dinner one evening, the husband was staring out of a window. I went over and stood by him. Suddenly he began to tell me all about it. He was a brilliant super-achiever whose wife had never seen the lonely little boy inside. When she had to spend a considerable amount of time in a hospital, and then still more time recovering her emotional stability at home, he found himself attracted to someone else. Though much younger than he, she knew how to mother him, something his "inner child" had apparently never received from either his mother or wife. Then his mistress betrayed him, and the lonely little boy-superman almost fell apart.

As he finished his story his wife joined us. He said, "I've just told him all about our problem." It was time for dinner, so I said, "Would you two like to talk about it after our evening session?" They both nodded.

That night we spent an hour together. When everything was out in the open, I said, "There is a sense in which neither of you is to blame. You were each reacting to normal human needs. If there were mistakes, they are in the past. From now on you are not to blame yourselves, or each other. The past is dead. That's what the cross is all about." I took her hand, and his, and told them more about this limitless, unconditional love of God as revealed in Christ.

Suddenly he reached over and took her hand, and mine. The three of us sat there, linked in a small circle of redemptive love. There was no one to forgive or to be forgiven. The past was dead. They walked away hand in hand. I had no assurance that their marriage would endure, but I sensed that whatever transpired, they would both be able to handle the situation with maturity, in the knowledge that "in everything God works for good with those who love him." [4]

Negative thinking holds onto the past, and refuses to forgive or start anew. The opposite attitude is one of love and trust—trust in the infinite love of God, whose we are, and who wants us to start each day anew.

Jesus said, "All things are possible to him who believes." [5] If you *can* believe in a loving God and a beneficent universe, many more things become possible than you ever dreamed of. Dreams can become realities. Your faith can make you sick—or whole.

> "Impatience is living in the future instead of the present." ANONYMOUS

3.
Give Me Patience Lord—
Right Now!

I DON'T KNOW WHETHER to feel amused or embarrassed when I recall that event in Dubrovnik, Yugoslavia. My wife and I were traveling behind the Iron Curtain, and had visited some of the major cities in the U.S.S.R., plus a half dozen other communist countries.

We decided to spend a few days at the exotic little city of Dubrovnik, Yugoslavia. Our plane arrived around eleven o'clock at night and we disembarked at a rather pleasant little airport. Then the trouble began.

Actually the difficulty was largely inside me, but I wasn't aware of it at the time. The passengers crowded together outside the airport waiting for their luggage. Two weary men carried each bag by hand from the plane to a bare spot on the ground behind a three-foot railing. I began to wonder, with mounting irritation, if the wheel had not yet been invented or discovered in Dubrovnik, since there seemed to be no hand trucks available.

There was some mild murmuring of discontent from the passengers as the men plodded back and forth from the plane to the mounting pile of luggage. It was nearing midnight when the two porters had the baggage all stacked in one huge mass five or six feet high. Then, as though they had achieved the first stage of some monumental victory, they smilingly invited the mob of tourists, in sign language, to point out their particular bags.

That did it! My adrenalin, which had slowly been gathering in some hidden pocket of my normally controlled personality, erupted. In good, clear authoritarian English I told them, for Heaven's sake, to spread the bags out so we could identify them. They listened uncomprehending. I pointed, gesticulated, explained in sign language. They seemed more puzzled than ever.

Finally one woman thought she had spotted her suitcase at the edge down near the bottom of the pile. Frantic scrambling resulted, and triumphantly one of the men handed her the bag. It was not hers after all. In the light of a naked forty watt bulb hanging from a pole twenty feet away it was hard to be sure of anything except a mass of people and the vast mound of luggage. The two porters tried again, pointing hopefully at the pile, and looking earnestly from face to face.

Now my adrenalin was off and running. I determined to help organize at least one aspect of a backward communist country. I strode back into the airport looking for an official. The place was deserted. Finally I found an amiable looking man standing nearby talking to some friends. I asked where the airport manager, or whoever was supposed to be in charge, could be found. Rather proudly, speaking in English, he said that he was the manager.

Then, my normal tact having deserted me, I demanded that he get the luggage mess straightened out. "At this rate," I told him, "we'll be here until 2:00 A.M. All they have to do is spread the bags out so people can identify them, take down the barrier, and in ten minutes it will all be over." He looked embarrassed and explained that the airport was new, and they were not yet well organized. "Then we'll organize it right now," I said, rather heatedly. He shrugged, and looked at his friends with some embarrassment. I had a momentary feeling of guilt over having criticized him in the presence of friends, but it was fleeting.

I walked back to the frustrated but apathetic crowd of tourists who seemed willing to wait all night for something to take place. Some were Europeans, the rest Americans. I wondered at their complacency. I leaped over the barricade and began to throw bags to the porters, pointing out where they were to put them in long lines so the passengers could identify their luggage. I was not just irritated, I was grossly indignant that in the latter part of the twentieth century such vast incompetence could exist. While all this was going on one phlegmatic American said to my wife, "Your husband gets kind of excited, doesn't he?" I don't recall her reply. She had seen this sort of thing happen before on rare occasions, and just smiled.

Finally I found our four bags and lugged them, two at a time, to the bus waiting to take us to the hotel. Triumphantly I sat down, and we waited in the empty bus. We waited another half hour while the rest of the passengers searched for their baggage and eventually got it aboard. Then we waited another twenty minutes for the bus driver. It was now around 1:00 A.M. and I wondered if the driver had defected to the West, leaving us stranded. Eventually he sauntered up in a leisurely fashion, and coaxed the ancient bus into action.

The bus stopped at a platform surrounded by a mass of porters. Now I knew why there were no porters at the airport. They were all waiting for us here. There must have been two to three porters for each passenger, scrambling, shouting, fighting over our bags. Finally I got one man to understand the name of our hotel. He carried the bags about fifteen feet and set them down beside a small hotel bus, and held out his hand. I had no local currency and handed him a dollar. Everyone in the world knows what a dollar is. I held out my hand for some change. He pocketed the bill and walked away.

I gave up and laughed. Either my adrenalin was all used up, or my sense of humor overcame my exasperation.

As I drifted off to sleep around 3:00 A.M. I realized that

my impatience, irritation and exasperation at human incompetence had produced nothing except a sense of utter
frustration. But Dubrovnik was beautiful, and by the next
morning all was forgiven. I could have patted Marshal Tito
on the shoulder and said, "I know you're doing your best, old
fellow. Just keep on trying."

When Should We Explode?

Now what has all this to do with prayer? Just this:

I learned as a very small child that anger was bad. It has
taken me most of my lifetime to learn at a feeling level that
all emotions are valid. Jesus did not tell us how to *feel*, but
how to *act*. I had not acted with my usual calm control
(which can be as phony as a three dollar bill). I had, with
some justification, let myself feel my exasperation. Despite
the fact that my actions were somewhat ridiculous, and
produced few if any positive results, I had at least let myself
feel something, instead of spending a lot of psychic energy
trying to pretend a poise and calm I did not feel. I decided to
evaluate it as neither good nor bad, but as "OK."

This raises a very important question: when are we to be
calm and patient, and when shall we let our indignation or
frustration be expressed?

Jesus cleansed the temple with a flaming moral indignation so violent that the hundreds of money changers and
traffickers in pigeons, sheep, and other sacrificial animals
were powerless before his onslaught. But there is one fact
which is seldom dealt with: we can be sure the money
changers and merchants were all back in business the next
day! The powerful politico-religious forces would not be af-
fected permanently by that one outburst of outrage. And, of
course, Jesus knew that his action constituted only a demon-
stration, from which there could not possibly be any permanent results. Must every act produce lasting results? I see
Jesus' moral indignation as so great that it had to be expressed, whether it made any permanent difference or not.

How can one know when to explode, and when to be self-contained? Where are the guidelines? Every distraught mother of small children who has screamed at her children must have wondered how much she is expected to endure. If, with iron will and stoic calm she controls her irritation, the children pick up the silent message on their tiny radars and react accordingly. Sometimes good, clean anger can be more creative than smoldering resentment. But how can you decide when to keep it in, and when to express it?

Your Life Script

I do not have any pat formula, but I have discovered a few hints along the way. My childhood "script" called for me to be a completely compliant "good boy"—a terrible thing to impose on a child. My anger all went underground and erupted in other ways. Displaced anger can manifest itself in physical and emotional symptoms, antisocial behavior, difficulty in functioning well in school or society, and in a score of other ways.

As an adult, still following my script, I normally present a calm exterior to the world; I do not maintain that this is either good or bad, only that it has a negative aspect to it. It is not always honest.

I was getting nowhere with a young woman in our counseling sessions. She had been the victim of a sadistic stepfather, and a mother who was incapable of expressing love. At an early age she left home to make it on her own, and was still trying to find her way when we began our counseling. It was unproductive. I couldn't reach her.

One day she said that she didn't trust me, because I was "always so calm and kind and accepting." She couldn't get to know me; she said, because I was "always the same, and no one is constantly like that inside." She couldn't trust me because I was, unconsciously, not being honest with her.

One evening in a Yokefellow group session I observed her sitting sprawled half asleep in her chair, seemingly indifferent to all that was going on. I felt something and expressed it. "Betty," I said, "it makes me angry when we offer you love and acceptance and you won't or can't accept it. I have given you unconditional acceptance, and you reject it. It's my problem, but I resent your unwillingness to respond." I put some feeling into it.

I could recall no other instance when I had not been my calm, clinical self in that group. But my feeling was genuine, and I expressed it. She waited until the others had left. Rather contritely and with a hurt look, she said, "I think I'll drop out of the group. I don't believe I belong." I gave her a hug and said, "Betty, I was honest with you, but I love you and want you in the group. Don't give up. We've just started being honest with each other." Betty did remain in the group. She could relate better to a feeling than to a façade.

There is a higher law than the law of honesty. It is the law of love. Love can help us gauge the ego strength of other persons, so that we do not crush them. Betty was not crushed. The next day she sent me an eight-page single-spaced autobiography. She listed everything she had ever done of which she was ashamed. There was plenty to feel guilty about, and at last she had gotten it all out. I had shown her an honest feeling and now she could be honest with me.

In our next counseling session I think she half feared that I would reject her totally, now that I knew the sordid side of her life. I told her that I liked her better for her complete honesty. The past was dead. She was not now the person who had blundered into all of those incredible messes. "In fact," I said, "I accept you totally, just as you are. God forgave you long ago. Now you must accept and forgive yourself."

In some indefinable way my honesty with her, even though it involved a negative expression, opened the door for her to be honest with me. She couldn't be real with me until I became real.

How Much Patience?

Now back to our original question, which has much to do

with prayer: how much patience is expected of us? "Love is patient and kind,"[1] wrote the Apostle Paul, but he and Barnabas had parted company after a violent disagreement. And Paul says that in an important controversy with Simon Peter, "I withstood him to the face."[2] Patience, then, does not imply perpetual placidity, either with people or with God.

We see the incredible patience of Jesus as he dealt with that motley assortment of twelve fishermen, tax collectors, and disillusioned revolutionaries. After three years of walking with him and hearing him speak to the multitudes, at the Last Supper when he entered the upper room they were quarreling over seating arrangements. The ones who considered themselves the most important members of the inner circle apparently wanted to be seated closest to him. How ridiculous, yet how human! Jesus' patience took an interesting form. Instead of lecturing them, he took a basin of water and a towel, and began to wash their feet. It was the function that a servant would perform for a dinner guest.

So, Jesus could loose the tempest of his indignation in the outer courtyard of the temple and drive out the squabbling merchants, and he could reveal exquisite tenderness and patience with these uncomprehending apostles, still shackled by their pride.

But *when* are we to be patient? When are we to be patient with people; when are we to refuse to put up with unacceptable behavior? One guideline is in a statement of Jesus, "If anyone wants to do God's will, he will know. . . ."[3] There is more to that statement, but one can safely say, "One who earnestly desires the will of God in his life can be sensitive enough to the guidance of the Spirit that *he will know the answer inwardly.*" God is seeking to guide us constantly. He is broadcasting love and forgiveness twenty-four hours a day. There is no need to plead for guidance—or anything else for that matter. We need only to get into harmony with his will. This means "conditioning the consciousness," getting quiet often enough so that the gentle whisper of guidance can be felt or perceived.

A professional woman told me that when her superior retired, a woman to whom she was greatly devoted, she was called upon to plan the farewell party. "I am no good at that sort of thing," she said, "and it created considerable anxiety in me, which I shared with a fellow worker." Her friend said, "I don't think it's the farewell party that's bothering you. It's something else."

"So," my friend said, "the next morning in my regular quiet time I emptied my mind and tried to let God tell me whatever it was he wanted me to hear. After a period of silence I suddenly became aware of what the problem was. It was not giving the farewell party that created all of that undue tension. It was the anxiety over the loss of my department head, and apprehension about who would succeed her. The message was as clear as a bell."

Be Still and Know

I do not know very many more difficult tasks than that of trying to get quiet every day for a period of meditation. I am an activist, and my script calls for me to be in motion. "Run and get me the hammer, son." "Run and bring me the ruler." "Run down to the store and get a loaf of bread." I seem to have heard that "Run and get me" message a hundred thousand times. I am still running.

When I sit or lie down to meditate I can hear that echo which now sounds like, "Get in motion. Get something done. Don't just sit there. Don't be lazy." So, it is only by an act of the will that I can take myself by the back of the neck, sit down and just "be." And when I do, and can let the motor slow down, I begin to get insights, ideas, messages, guidance.

"Be still, and know that I am God," [4] could be translated, "Be still, and you can know God and hear his quiet message." "In quietness and in trust shall be your strength"[5] can also mean, "As you learn to get quiet, you will find your answers."

There are cathedrals in Europe which took hundreds of years to complete. A guide in Cologne, Germany, told me that construction on their great cathedral went on for nine hundred years. This seems incredible in an age when a skyscraper is completed in a year or so at the most. I have a profound admiration for the patience of people to whom twenty or thirty generations were not too long to wait for the completion of a magnificent cathedral.

But, as stated before, any virtue pushed to its extreme can become a vice. If I were a Black being counseled to have patience and to wait another generation or two—or a decade for that matter—for racial equality, I would be more than indignant. Every sane person hates war, yet we revere the heroes of the Revolutionary War, whose patience was finally exhausted.

I cannot solve the world's problems, but I do have a responsibility to order my life so that I will, to the best of my ability, love God with all my nature, love my neighbor, and learn to love myself properly. These are lofty, unattainable goals, rather than rigid requirements. But the goal itself provides the basic guidelines for life. It can take a lifetime to make significant progress in this.

Patience, in the matter of prayer, is related to the whole question of when to "possess your soul in patience," and when to "put on the whole armor of God" and set things right. Only God can guide us in each individual instance.

Upon accepting the pastorate of my second church, where I spent thirty-four happy years, I found a hopelessly inadequate church constitution. It was a patchwork quilt of committees piled on committees, with no single board having any real authority. I insisted upon a new form of church organization. Within a month we had completed a new constitution which worked so successfully that over three hundred other churches subsequently adopted it.

On the other hand, I waited twenty-five years to accomplish one relatively minor change in the church procedure. About every three to five years I would bring it before the board. Usually there would be some mild to strong objection, whereupon I always suggested that we table the matter. It may have been some perverse stubborn streak in me, since no important principle was involved, but I kept bringing the matter up. Finally after twenty-five years, when I suggested the change, the general reaction was, "Why, this is a splendid idea! Why has it not been presented to us before?" Of course, there had been many changes in the board membership during those years. It passed unanimously.

We Are Neither Patient nor Impatient—But Both

In a sense I am amused at my persistence over a fairly minor issue; yet I see some of this same "patient-impatient" ambivalence in most people. Depending on our mood or metabolism or genetic wiring, many of us seem to display both qualities at different times. The Apostle Paul could endure untold hardship—whether in prison, being shipwrecked or stoned by his enemies—but when he is criticized by the church in Corinth for his poor preaching and weak personality, he understandably reacts with something less than a calm patience.[6] He quite properly justifies himself to the best of his ability. I think being shipwrecked would be preferable to being told that you had a weak personality and couldn't preach very well!

When you have prayed and waited, and kept on praying, and no answer has been forthcoming, how much longer should you wait? In one of our Yokefellow retreats, a woman said that she had been praying and waiting for twenty years for her husband to love her. He did love her in his own way, but never having known love as a child, he was literally incapable of expressing it. Her question, "How long must I wait?" has come echoing down the centuries: "How long, O Lord, how long?" In the next chapter we will deal with some specific means and methods, but I would like to close this chapter with a general formula: "When you learn to love God with all your heart, and want his will above all else, you will know the answer."

"Honesty with oneself, with God and others is
the all-essential first step to effective prayer."
C. GILLETTE

4.
Formulas
for Effective Prayer

"I REALIZE THAT THIS sounds sort of odd," said Mary Lou,
"but I have to kill my mother."

I was not too surprised that Mary Lou felt intense
hostility toward her mother, but her calm statement
startled me. Her distraught parents had brought her to me
three years before when she was thirteen, and out of control. The mother was a sweet, overly compliant woman with
a pained, martyred voice. She told how earnestly she had
prayed that Mary Lou might give up her defiant, rebellious
ways and "act normal." The mother had been the frequent
victim of Mary Lou's violent verbal and physical attacks.

The father was a phlegmatic man who delivered tedious,
interminable moralistic lectures in a flat monotone. Both
he and his wife were surprised when I suggested that they
come in for regular counseling. "But it's Mary Lou, Dr.
Osborne. She's the one who's in trouble. We pray and do
everything we can, so why don't we just go on praying
and you see what you can do to get her straightened out?"

But I was insistent on seeing the parents too, and over a
lengthy period of time we made some slight progress. Mary
Lou was wild, incorrigible, in trouble at school as well as
at home. She communicated with me only in monosyllables
for months. Eventually things got a little better. The

46

mother phoned one day to say that her prayers had been answered. "It's just like heaven compared to what it has been in the past. Prayer does change people, doesn't it?" I warned the mother that we had really only begun, and that much more time was needed to make the changes permanent. The father had not given up his lecturing, and the mother was still, though to a lesser degree, complaining about minor symptomatic behavior. The parents needed help as much as Mary Lou. But, as the mother saw it, the "magic" of prayer had worked; Mary Lou stopped coming for counseling.

A few months later she ran away from home, after a two-hour session with her martyred mother and lecturing father. She ended up in the most vice-ridden section of San Francisco where she lived with five men, all drug addicts, for nearly two weeks. She was on drugs of one kind or another the entire time. When finally the police and her parents found her, she was brought in to see me. It was then that she said, without any emotion, "I have to kill my mother." She had blown her mind, at least for the time being. I recommended that she be sent to a psychiatric hospital for intensive treatment. For the next few years, during which I did not see her on a counseling basis, she made some slight progress. At eighteen she married a boy no more mature than she, and of course the marriage was a disaster.

So much for trying to "change" someone else through prayer—and for short-term therapy.

We Cannot Change Others

It is nowhere recommended in the Bible that we try to change anyone else. Pray for them, yes; change them, no. What right do I have to try to change someone else to fit my concept of what he should be like? Even God will not exercise his power to change us against our wills. He makes it *our* responsibility to change ourselves. His resources are available, but he will not force or control us.

The wife of an alcoholic said in one of our Yokefellow groups that she had prayed for years that her husband would stop drinking, a seemingly valid plea. "But," she added, "I was unaware at the time that I was masochistic, a martyr of the worst kind. I didn't realize that I triggered most of his drinking bouts with my complaints." It took her a long time to come to the realization that subconsciously she *needed* to be abused. Consciously she had wanted a sober husband who would treat her kindly. Unconsciously she had wanted to be punished for unresolved guilt feelings originating in the distant past, and long since buried.

"I no longer pray for my husband to stop drinking," she told us. "I pray about my own attitudes. If I can bring them into harmony with the spirit of Christ, I will be a better wife, with no unconscious need to be punished or abused. If he changes, as I hope he will, it will be on his own initiative. I am not trying to change him. I am in the process of changing myself."

Before we deal with the conditions for effective prayer, let's examine some of the reasons for the ineffectiveness of the prayers of Mary Lou's parents. Their mistakes were very common ones:

First, their prayers had to do with trying to change their daughter, not themselves.

Second, they focused on the problem, and became problem-centered. All they could talk about or pray about was the symptomatic problem.

Third, they were never able to visualize Mary Lou as whole. They hoped for it, of course, but chiefly they focused on her excessive makeup, how she fixed her hair, the length of her skirts, her language, and the negative aspects of her personality.

Fourth, they were giving Mary Lou a daily message which was, "You're not okay. We cannot accept you as you are." So she continued rebelling, fulfilling the "not okay" script her parents gave her.

Fifth, they had a very immature and simplistic concept

of how prayer works. They told God how bad Mary Lou was, and how much they hoped she would change, but in so doing they were "praying to the problem."

Sixth, Mary Lou was rebelling against everything her parents represented: a moralizing, lecturing father, and a mother trying to impose 1935 manners, dress and attitudes on her.

Seventh, they vacillated between being overly permissive and excessively authoritarian. They could not seem to grasp the idea that there is a third alternative, midway between permissiveness and authoritarianism.

The principles involved in the unhappy story of Mary Lou and her parents have a general application. To begin with, prayer should never be used to change another person. We do not have the right to change or control anyone. In the case of a small child there is the obligation to provide an atmosphere in which there are ample opportunities for growth. There need to be well-defined limits, which should be consistent. But we have no right to change the child, to make him over into what we think he should be like. It is possible and often desirable to change or control a child's destructive course of *action*, but this does not necessarily change the child.

Startling as it may sound at first, there is a sense in which *I am not responsible to or for any other person.* The Bible does not declare that I am to be my brother's keeper. That idea was voiced in the form of a question by Cain who, when God asked about his brother, snarled, "Am I my brother's keeper?" [1] I am my brother's *brother*, not his keeper.

No, we are not responsible *for* one another or *to* one another; we are responsible only to *love* each other. To feel responsible for other persons implies that we must somehow control them or make them over, get them to see things our way, or to order their lives. This is nowhere commanded or even suggested by Jesus.

Since so much of our praying has to do with children,

parents, friends, and associates, I have gone into the matter of relationships at some length. Now we can deal with some basic principles underlying effective prayer.

Principles of Effective Prayer

Naturally you will pray when and where you feel like it: in church, on the bus, or in a quiet time set aside for a regular time of communion with God. The suggested principles I am outlining here are only general guidelines. The prayer life of each individual may vary from day to day and at different times of life. Here is a series of suggestions which can be used in any way that seems to fit your own personality and individual needs.

First, operate on the assumption that you are not responsible to or for any other person. This relieves you of the futile urge to change others, or the feeling that you should let another control you.

Second, try to accept the concept that the only person you can change is yourself. Assuming that you are ten percent at fault, and can get credible witnesses to verify that the other person is ninety percent wrong, the only portion you are responsible to change is your ten percent. If you have difficulty accepting this idea, I suggest that you skip this chapter. Unless you can abandon the idea of changing other people, you may waste a vast amount of time in futile prayer, and make numerous people unhappy with you.

Third, try to find a place where you can be alone and quiet every day. If music helps create the proper mood, whether it be sacred, classical or popular, by all means use this or any other means of achieving a state of consciousness conducive to meditation and reflection.

Fourth, try to find a particular *time* of the day when you can be quiet. This does require a certain amount of discipline, but nothing significant was ever achieved without some form of discipline. However, if you are the type of person who enjoys keeping up a kind of running conversation with God throughout the day, then that might be your best approach. However, for some of us that can be a cop-out, a rationalization to avoid having a specific time during which we examine our own souls, our motives, our relationships, and our goals.

Fifth, condition the consciousness, or to put it differently, practice relaxing your body, then your mind. Let your face muscles relax; then your neck and shoulders, then your back and entire torso. Visualize all of the accumulated tensions draining out of you. Let your mind focus on various parts of the body, inviting them to let go. Involuntary muscles will continue to relax as you quietly give them instructions to release their tension. The mind and spirit function better in a relaxed body. It may take anywhere from five to fifteen minutes or more to achieve adequate physical relaxation through suggestion, but it is worth whatever time it takes. It is part of the command: "Be still and know."

Sixth, let your mind relax, along with your body. As you empty your mind of tensions and anxieties, significant things can happen. For instance, recently I lay down for fifteen minutes and listened to some music to clear the channels of my mind, after consciously letting my entire body relax. My mind became almost a complete blank.

Then there arose a feeling or thought, "I hate my father!" *My word! Where did that come from? He's been dead for years!*

I let my mind wander, unhindered by conscious direction. What was it about my father that I disliked? Well, it was his frown which, as a child, I mistook for disapproval, not realizing. that it was partly from personal worries. I disliked his critical, negative attitude, and his judgmental spirit. Then without any conscious effort to control my thinking, I realized that those are some of the things I dislike about myself, as I dislike them in anyone else.

My mind wandered farther afield. I hated poverty and crime; I hated war and pain and suffering and a score of other things that came surging up. I let myself feel pure hate of all that is evil and wrong with man and his world. Then arose the feeling, "I hate myself, too, because I am part of the world's pain and suffering."

Having learned as a child that "It's wrong to hate," I have had to learn to let myself feel hostile emotions without judging them as bad.

Then came another feeling. It was the feeling of "hurt"— the world's hurts. I was angry and hostile because there is so much pain and hurt in the world. So I let my mind range through the teeming ghettos of the world; through the streets of Calcutta where a hundred thousand people lie down in the streets at night, never having had a home. I remembered the million Palestinian Arab refugees driven from their homes, most of them still living in refugee camps, subsisting on eight cents a day worth of grain handed out by UNRRA. My mind wandered through the corridors of mental hospitals, where tens of thousands are locked up. Then I thought of the hurts of parents with malformed children, and the pitiful child-creatures who are mentally deficient, and will never know joy or pleasure or fulfillment.

In those few brief minutes my mind roamed the whole world and felt the diffused pain and hurt of mankind. And then everything came into focus on a hill, where stood three crosses. On the center cross hung a man with arms outstretched, as though to say, "Come unto me, all of you who are hurting from whatever cause, and I will love you and give you rest from your pain." It was only after I had felt hate and anger, followed by my own hurts and those of the world, that I could feel love. I felt something of the redemptive love of God who does not will our pain, but longs for us to love one another enough, so that the well can help the suffering, and the strong the weak.

Start with Your Anger

It's difficult to diagram emotion, but I perceive it something like this:

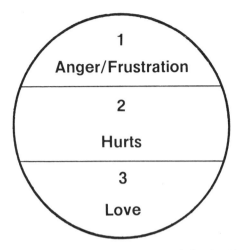

A fundamental psychological principle is that a frustrated child reacts with anger or rage. Anyone who is hurting emotionally or physically feels resentment, anger, frustration, or some combination of these emotions. There is really nothing wrong with any of us, or the world, except hurts. These came from inadequate environmental conditions in childhood, and genetic deficiencies. Because we hurt, we are angry. That anger will be either turned outward in some form of aggression, or inward in the form of self-hate, producing a host of emotional symptoms ranging from depression to insanity, or physical symptoms of a hundred different kinds.

Spiritually and psychologically it is sometimes better to start with your anger or frustration. If the psalmists could do it with profit to themselves spiritually, you can feel justified in doing it. There is no need to deny your feelings. They are neither good nor bad—they are just feelings and you are entitled to feel whatever emotion you experience. How you *act* is another matter.

At times, when you pray, start with your irritations, your frustrations, your anger, perhaps even rage. Let the feelings up! There is nothing wrong with hate! Everyone hates. It can be your job, your marriage, your children, your frustrations. *Express* your feelings!

Then move into your hurts, and the hurts of the world. Feel your own and others'. Identify with those whose condition is worse than your own. Letting yourself feel compassion for the suffering people of the world is in itself an act of prayer for all who suffer. Then let yourself feel your own pain or frustration. This is not self-pity unless it becomes a habit. What's so wrong with feeling a little sympathy for the suffering self? Have as much compassion for yourself as you would for another person with similar problems.

Then, when you have let yourself feel your anger, and your hurts, you can tap that vast reservoir of love that God has built into every human being. It's there, deep down, ready to be experienced when the anger and fear and hurts have all been felt out.

"Faith working through love," [2] is a phrase Paul used in his letter to the Galatians. Put another way, "You will have more faith when you learn how to love properly." So, get out the anger, feel the hurts, then let your soul bathe in the limitless love of God. Finally, you will be ready to engage in another aspect of prayer. What you have been doing so far is prayer, too; for whenever you turn your attention to God, or lovingly toward his creatures, you are praying. If in quiet reflection, with a sense that God is nearby, you look within to find some hurt or anger, you are praying.

Look for Barriers

Now begin to look for barriers. Besides hate or resentment, the basic ones are a sense of inferiority, fear and guilt. Start with guilt. In what way do you feel guilty? Deal with faulty attitudes, not merely the deeds. Faulty actions are usually only symptomatic end-results of wrong attitudes. Instead of confessing the sin, confess the sinful self. "This is what I am, Lord, and I will probably remain this way until I receive some divine help to grow beyond my present limited self." Follow the symptom back to the source, the impaired self. Share that with God. Guilt is the most destructive of all emotions. It destroys relationships between you and God, and between you and others. It must be dealt with, confessed, then abandoned.

In a later chapter we will deal with guilt and prayer, offering some specific techniques for achieving self-forgiveness, as well as God's forgiveness.

Now deal with inferiority. Everyone experiences feelings of this type, because in some ways we are all inferior or deficient. Inferiority is closely related to guilt at a feeling level. Instead of focusing upon the areas of your inferiority, list your positive qualities, and thank God for them. In the process make sure that your sense of inferiority is not producing some neurotic symptoms. We tend to compensate for our sense of inferiority. There are legitimate and creative ways of dealing with inferiority feelings, and there are sneaky ways.

One creative way of handling inferiority is to try to achieve something which will give you a sense of worth. The less creative ways are numerous: name-dropping, compulsive talking, the use of attention-getting devices, the need to gain power over people so as to control them, and, of course, carping criticism. The worst critic is nearly always the one who feels the most inferior. Many people possessed of great talent have a deep sense of inferiority originating in childhood. Unless this sense is dealt with constructively, it can manifest itself as pomposity, hypersensitivity, argumentativeness or just plain obnoxiousness.

A man endowed with a brilliant intellect and outstanding talents had not related well with his peer group as a boy. As an adult he spoke brilliantly, wrote well, achieved distinctions and honors in scores of ways, but he always remained at heart the lonely little boy who felt rejected as a child. Because he could not deal with his deep childhood hurts, his personality was marred by neurotic traits which clearly revealed his deep insecurities.

So when you come to pray, take time for introspection. Review the hurts, the feelings of inferiority, the guilt, the anger—and offer the whole self to God. Now at last you are ready for some other forms of prayer—gratitude, adoration, petition, intercessory prayer—or for silent fellowship and communion with the Father. (Elsewhere we deal with reasons why some people should never pray to God, or use the word "Father" as applied to God, but should pray rather to Jesus.)

Prayer should not be stereotyped, or it can become monotonous. There are times when you will want to visualize something on your mental screen and become a cocreator with God by letting that visualization become a reality. If you can visualize something deeply enough, you can realize it.

Then there is the matter of relinquishment. When you have prayed something through, and have done everything you feel led to do, this can be the time to relinquish the problem. Verbalize it, visualize it as accomplished, and "hang it on a hook" over on the left side of your mind, on the periphery of your attention. It will float back into attention from time to time. If you get no new insights, put it back on the hook and let God deal with it. Here is where patience comes in, and patience is closely related to trust and faith.

Prayer is not magic. The inner child of the past, still resident within us, would really like a kind of celestial Santa Claus who would "make all the bad people good, and all the good people nice," and send us a lot of goodies. The impatient child within likes instantaneous cures, quick magic, simplistic answers. Personally I would go for that button-pushing kind of magic in a big way. It's easy, and requires no growth or real responsibility on my part. The child part of me would like to achieve spiritual growth without effort.

But the more mature, adult self recognizes that there are conditions which must be met. There must be honesty with God, self, and others. There must be intensity of desire. Continuity is a third important factor. One may continue in prayer until he discovers that perhaps he has been praying amiss, for the wrong thing, or with the wrong attitude. Or, if he has not failed at any of these points, there is always the possibility that his impatience wants instant results, whereas God, in his infinite wisdom, sees that the time may not be ripe.

A Biblical Formula for Prayer

There is a biblical formula for prayer expressed in such beautiful, poetic language that the tendency is to admire it for its beauty of expression, and ignore the fact that it is an explicit, down-to-earth formula for answered prayer:

Agree with God and be at peace;
    thereby good shall come to you. . . .
If you return to the Almighty and humble yourself,
    if you remove unrighteousness far from your tents, . . .
and if you will delight yourself in the Almighty,
    and lift up your face to God.
You will make your prayer to him, . . .
    and you will pay your vows.
[Then] you will decide on a matter, and it will be established
      for you,
    and light will shine on your ways.

JOB 22:21-28

Now suppose we paraphrase that:

    Get into harmony with God's cosmic principles and
        you will be at peace;
      then good things will happen to you.
    If you will return to the Father, and be very humble
        and receptive,
      and live as righteous a life as you can;
    if you learn to delight in having communion with God,
      and make good on your commitments,
    Then, *anything you decide upon will come to pass.*

There it is in black and white, step by step. Seek to discover the cosmic, universal principles through which God works. Get in harmony with them, and you will have inner peace, which is his will for you. Righteousness suggests a right relationship with God and man. Do as well as you can in this area. When you no longer fear God or his will in your life, but have learned to enjoy his presence and to talk to him as friend to friend; and when you have fulfilled all of your commitments to the best of your ability, whatever you ask for you will receive.

Is that too big an order? Perhaps it may be for the moment. But you can start. And to the degree that you fulfill those conditions, your prayers will be answered.

5.
Steps in Practical Prayer

HOW CAN WE BE SURE that our prayers will be effective? To answer that question, suppose we consider some (though surely not all) of the major steps in practical prayer. Let me just list them first. The order is not of primary importance, though for some people such a priority can be of value.

1. *Seek to love God more than his gifts.* When you achieve this, as Meister Eckhart points out, "you may have all else besides." You may have prosperity and health, but they will not exalt you; or, you may have poverty and/or ill health, but they will not defeat you.

2. *Express gratitude for present blessings before seeking additional ones.*

3. *Confess not only the symptomatic sins or failures but the impaired self.*

4. *Cultivate unselfishness by praying for others first.* "Thy kingdom come, Thy will be done, On earth," precedes "Give us this day our daily bread." [1]

5. *Seek guidance, in all humility, concerning what to pray about.* "You ask and do not receive, because you ask wrongly," James reminds us.[2]

6. *Desire with all your heart the things you seek.* "You will seek me and find me; when you seek me with all your

heart." [3] Intensity of desire is an important prerequisite to effective prayer.

7. *Visualize what it is that you desire, and see it as accomplished.* If you can visualize it, you can realize it.

8. *Be willing to have it so—whether your request is granted or not.* We often pray, in our human fallibility, for things which God in love and wisdom cannot grant us.

9. *Let the prayer be positive, affirming what you know to be true about God and life.*

10. *Relinquish the desire once you have prayed it through.* We are "not heard for our much speaking." Turn the desire over to the Father in perfect childlike trust, doubting nothing.

11. *Be prepared to act upon any insights gained while in communion with the Father.*

12. *Keep in tune, making prayer a regular, daily communion with God, who wants our fellowship more than he desires our service.*

Do these twelve steps make it sound too complicated? Perhaps at first it may seem so, but in time one needs no outline, or list of successive steps. You buy a new car and are, of course, totally unfamiliar with all of the new gadgetry on the dash. You study the manual, figure out which device does what, and in time it all becomes instinctive. So it is with the steps in prayer.

Let us take up the twelve steps in order, considering each one in more detail.

1. *Love God more than his gifts.*

After the Second World War, the church of which I was senior minister sponsored a dozen or more refugees. The first one was assigned to us more or less at random. We were informed that the man being sent us, together with his wife and six-year-old son, was a Ukrainian woodchopper. I thought, "What in the world will we do with a Ukrainian woodchopper in a prosperous suburban area of San Francisco!"

When the little family arrived, their only possessions a

few pitiful bundles of clothing, the husband announced his name, "Me Vladimir Wdowich." Since I couldn't pronounce his name, I said, "You *Joe*," and Joe he has remained to this day.

Joe spoke no English, but he had a good grasp of German, and we communicated at first through a man in the church who spoke German. We had just lost our janitor, so Joe was put to work as church custodian.

To my amazement he seemed to sense what to do without being told. In the twenty-five years he served as custodian I am sure I didn't give him a dozen instructions. Joe handled his money very wisely. In a short time he had a savings account. Within a year or so he had saved and borrowed enough for the down payment on a small house. His wife found a job nearby.

Joe could have left us for a better paying job at any time after the first year. Instead, out of gratitude, he remained with us. Everyone loved him, and he loved everyone, old and young.

During the first few years he sent over $10,000 worth of clothing to relatives in Russia. Later he organized a Ukrainian Baptist church, which still meets in the church chapel. They have their own minister and a fine congregation.

Twenty-five years from the time Joe arrived, penniless and frightened, he owns a $52,000 home with a very small mortgage on it; a $325,000 apartment house on which he owes only $130,000. He plans to retire at fifty-five.

Joe did not come to America to get rich, but to survive and be free. He never prayed for or sought great prosperity. His chief goal in life was to serve God and man, out of love and deep gratitude. His comparative prosperity is a by-product, not a primary goal. He would have been a loving, compassionate, happy man even if he hadn't been financially successful.

Trust and love are twin sisters. There can be no deep love without trust. At a Sunday morning service when the time came for the children's sermon, I stepped down in front of the group of children, holding a sheaf of $1.00 bills in my hand. "I have a one dollar bill to give to any of you who will come up and ask for it," I told them. "Of course, you will have to run the risk that I may ask for it back after the service. You will have to trust me when I say I won't do that. You could be embarrassed in some way if you step up here to get your dollar. I don't know how much you trust me not to embarrass you. Here is the money. Will anyone come?"

Instantly, Becky, a lovely little blonde girl, came up, took her dollar, thanked me, and sat down. This encouraged two other girls to come. I waited. Several boys were chewing their fingernails. I watched one in particular. His father had abandoned him. He knew me quite well, but—he had been hurt very badly. I waited. No one else came. Becky had learned to trust and to love, as had the other two girls; but each of the others had somehow learned that people can't be trusted.

Our capacity to trust and love God seems to bear a relationship to our childhood experiences. A child who learns that adults cannot be trusted usually finds it difficult to trust either man or God in later life. And how can one love a God whom he does not fully trust? One can learn to trust by trial and error. Faith works through love, we read.[4] Love is based on trust and faith.

2. *Express gratitude for present blessings before seeking additional ones.*

Jesus once healed ten lepers, who rushed off to the priests for the required verification of their healing. But one turned back impetuously to thank him. Jesus said, "Were not ten cleansed? Where are the nine?"[5] Jesus did not need the gratitude of the other nine. But there is something wrong with ungrateful people. *They* are the losers.

In the same sense there is something wrong with us when our prayers consist almost solely of petitions. I counseled with a man for five or six years in an effort to help him overcome the results of some very traumatic childhood experiences, as well as some errors of his own. I was so gratified at his steady growth and final success that it did not occur to me until much later that he had never expressed any word of gratitude for the years of help he had received. I felt no need of his gratitude, but I did feel that his inability to express appreciation represented a flaw in his personality.

Meister Eckhart insists that gratitude is one of the greatest of virtues. If so, lack of gratitude could be one of the greater of the sins.

Before you seek God's blessings, list all the things for which you are grateful. Are you thankful for life and health? For the country in which you live? For your material blessings? For friends, family? For music and beauty and laughter? For ample food in a world where one-third of the world goes to bed hungry, and another third is inadequately fed? You might make out a written list. "Count your many blessings, name them one by one / And it will surprise you what the Lord hath done," [6] as an old hymn has it.

3. *Confess, not only the symptomatic sins or failures, but the impaired self.*

I no longer confess the individual errors I make, the things I term symptomatic sins. They are merely symptoms of some deeper spiritual failure in my life. The sin, or mistake, or failure or whatever, brings a sense of shame or guilt. Then I trace the act or failure back to the warped or limited attitude and say, "Lord, this is what I am, and I confess it. I will probably remain this way without your help. I seek that help now."

Suppose a compulsive eater, or a compulsive drinker, or someone with a hair-trigger temper, were to confess after each failure. Nothing is accomplished except that the person feels still more guilty. It would be better if such an individual were to ask, "What is there in me that makes me act this way, and what can I do to overcome my problem?" I do not doubt that some personality disorders have been healed instantaneously in response to prayer, but more often such persons seem to require a trained counselor who can help dig out the hidden roots of the difficulty.

When the body malfunctions most of us lose no time in looking up a physician. The same principle applies to any impairment of personality. If there is a spiritual or emotional problem one is wise to pray for guidance in seeking a suitable counselor—minister, psychologist, psychiatrist —or some objective person skilled in this particular kind of personality malfunction.

4. *Cultivate unselfishness by praying for others first.*

In the Lord's prayer we are taught not even to ask for a crust of bread until we have earnestly prayed:

> Our Father who art in heaven,
> Hallowed be thy name.
> Thy kingdom come,
> Thy will be done
> On earth, as it is in heaven.[7]

I cannot utter those words without seeing in a flash all of the lonely, hungry, deprived, suffering people of earth. My concern for them, perhaps finally narrowed down to some one such person near at hand, can cause me to ask, "Lord, what would you have me do about this person whose face now comes before me?"

Since faith works by love, if I love God I will manifest it by expressing love for specific individuals. Only as I love, and express it, can I acquire faith.

5. *Seek guidance, in all humility, concerning what to pray about.*

Sometimes it is best not to rush into God's presence breathlessly with a shopping list. *Wait!* "Be still, and know. . . ." [8] Get quiet and in a state of "wantlessness." Your impatience will prompt you to verbalize your needs and petitions. But wait and let him speak to you. When I do this, invariably I receive some awareness or insight that was farthest from my conscious mind; yet the insight always makes sense.

6. *Desire with all your heart the things you seek.*

My emotions range from irritation to exasperation when I hear a public prayer which encompasses "every continent, the islands of the sea, those suffering on beds of pain, the impoverished and the lonely, the nations at war, the fatherless and the widow," and to top it off, "all for whom we should pray." I doubt if such a prayer does any harm. It might just possibly turn some listener's attention in a less selfish direction. But my mind wanders, and I feel the prayer is a form of wishful thinking rather than earnest supplication.

I had a friend in college who shared with me the fact that he wanted to "make a lot of money, and do a lot of good in the world." Forty years later he had achieved neither goal. He had split motives. Besides, his priorities were wrong. He desired wealth so that life would be pleasant. Doing "a lot of good in the world" seemed to be a pious afterthought.

A mountain climber scaling Mt. Everest does not simultaneously seek fame and wealth and ease and education and a perfect marriage. *All* of his mental and physical resources are focused upon one objective—to reach the mountaintop. He seeks that one goal with all his heart.

"Where your treasure is, there will your heart be also," [9] Jesus told his disciples. It might also be said, "Where you are *hurting*, there is where your heart is." If you are deeply concerned about, or hurting for, a friend or relative, or yourself, your prayer is much more earnest—thus more effective—than if you deal with pious generalities.

Intensity of desire seems to be a vital aspect of effective prayer. It focuses one's diffused attention upon the concern at hand.

7. *Visualize what it is that you desire, and see it as accomplished. If you can visualize it, you can realize it.*

A father reported that every night when he heard his

young son's prayer, he prayed also. Usually he added, "and make Jimmy a good boy." One night he suddenly realized what a wretched prayer that was! It implied that Jimmy was *not* a good boy. Besides he was setting up a standard no one can ever reach—being "good" all the time.

He changed his prayer to one of positive affirmation thereafter: "and thank you Lord for making Jimmy such a fine boy." Thus he was affirming his small son, and at the same time visualizing him as continuing to be a fine boy in the future.

8. *Be willing to have it so.*

This phrase is one used by William James, father of modern psychology, and a profound Christian. He once said in a lecture that "to be willing to have it so is the first step in solving any problem."

The phrase also applies to prayer. Having prayed, I am not always certain that the things I have sought are a part of God's will. So I usually add, "Lord, I am finite. You are infinite. You know whether what I seek is right under the circumstances. If I am wrong in wanting this, I gladly accept no for an answer. I want my requests to be in harmony with your glorious, wonderful will."

I was about to graduate from the seminary. Certain that God had called me into the ministry, I was also confident that it was up to him to guide me to the right church upon graduation. I was the youngest graduate, and feeling the least well qualified, I envisioned a small-town church some place nearby in Kentucky or Indiana. I preached for a number of little churches and got only negative responses.

As graduation day approached, I told God that he'd have to hurry things up if he wanted me in the ministry. "Any church will do, Lord, even the smallest. But it's up to you. I've done my part."

A day or two later I received an invitation from a splendid Chicago church to preach for them. I did so and returned with no expectation of hearing anything further from them. The best I could hope for would be a little crossroads church. Then came the greatest surprise of my life. The outstanding Chicago church with a fine congregation, a lovely building, and no indebtedness, extended me an enthusiastic and unanimous call to become their pastor. I still have that forty-two-year-old letter, though I am not a sentimentalist.

Apparently I had fulfilled at least a few of the conditions: I could visualize pastoring *some* church, though my expectation was far below what God provided. And I am grateful that I was "willing to have it so"—meaning, whatever God willed was going to be all right.

9. *Let the prayer be positive, affirming what you know to be true about God and life.*

I love the assertion of Paul, who tells us that God "is able to do far more abundantly than all that we ask or think." [10] Another writer asks rhetorically, "Is anything too hard for the Lord?" [11]

The sun is so large that, if it were hollow, it could contain more than a million worlds the size of our earth. But there are stars out there in space, astronomers tell us, that could hold 500 million suns the size of ours. Add to that fact that there are at least 100 million galaxies in known space, each galaxy containing more than 100 billion stars. What an unimaginably vast operation God has set in motion! Yet, God is as concerned about the broken wing of a sparrow as he is with those billions of stars in a distant galaxy.

When you pray you need not consider yourself or your needs as unimportant. Each atom in the universe receives the same loving consideration given the greatest constellation. Every human being on earth, however faulty or fallen, merits the love and attention of God. He loves all that he has made, and undoubtedly he loves most that portion of himself which he has planted deep within each of us. He loves you, not because you are *good*, but because you are *his*.

When you pray affirm this to yourself. Remind yourself of Jesus' invitation, "Come to me, all who labor and are heavy-laden. . . ." [12] Don't focus upon your alleged unworthiness. Focus upon God's infinite love, revealed in Christ.

10. *Relinquish the desire, once you have prayed it through.*

Perhaps you have prayed for weeks, months, or years for something you desired. Or you prayed, did not receive an affirmative answer, and gave up. Giving up is not the same as relinquishment.

I was touring Mexico with my family, and unexpected car repairs of major proportions used up most of my available cash. Neither the garage nor the local bank would accept my check. I wired a friend of mine at home for two hundred dollars. Having sent the telegram I relinquished the problem, secure in the knowledge that I could trust my friend to send me the money. It arrived the next day. I knew he had the money, and that he would consider it a pleasure to be of help; and most of all, I trusted him. Our relationship had been a long one. We knew each other well.

If you and God have established such a relationship, you can claim the promise, "If you abide in me, and my words abide in you, ask whatever you will, and it shall be done for you." [13]

11. *Be prepared to act upon any insights gained while in communion with the Father.*

Some years ago I was suffering from excessive fatigue. I knew vaguely that it was from overwork, but tried to keep this idea out of consciousness. In a quiet time one day I let God do all the talking, after I had asked for a solution to my problem.

The response was startlingly brief: *"Rest, exercise, and prayer constitute the formula."* Rather compulsively, however, I kept to my old schedule, going where I was pushed instead of setting my own pace. I planned to get some exercise, but kept postponing it. I settled for prayer, which was cheating, for it comprised only one-third of the formula. I asked for an answer, received it, and failed to act on the guidance.

There is almost no limit to the number of rationalizations one can employ in an effort to justify a predetermined course. I used them all. Only lately, years after I sought an answer and got it, have I begun to *act* on the guidance I received. I was not punished for disregarding the guidance, but the results—more fatigue—were just about as severe as punishment might have been. However, they were consequences, not punishment, since God does not punish.

12. *Keep in tune, making prayer a regular, daily communion with God, who wants our fellowship more than he desires our service.*

One might use a dozen terms to describe what is meant by "keeping in tune." Use any phrase or word that fits your need. "A quiet time" may sound a bit pious to some, or have other negative connotations. "Plugging into the cosmic power of God" could sound slightly irreverent to some, but practical to others. Call it meditation, prayer, communion, fellowship with God, or anything you choose when you look within to seek the Source of your being, or look heavenward, or feel gratitude welling up within you, or simply quiet your restless mind so that God can speak to you in the silence. You are praying.

For, stated simply, prayer is bringing all of yourself that you can be aware of, into fellowship with all of God that you understand. At that point God rejoices and accepts you.

6.
God Wills Wholeness of Body, Mind, and Circumstance

AT THE OPENING SESSION of a retreat several years ago, I observed a depressed-looking young woman seated on the front row. Not once during the entire afternoon did she lift her eyes from the floor. During a half-hour break be-fore dinner, someone told me, "That young woman wants to talk to you, but she's afraid to ask you."

I went up to the young woman and asked if she would care to go for a walk with me. I sensed that she might feel more at ease if she didn't have to sit facing me. As we walked along a country road, I tried to discover the nature of her problem.

Dully she reported that she had been in four different mental institutions, that she was married and had several small children. The diagnosis, she said, had been schizo-phrenia.

"That's just a psychiatric catchall phrase," I said. "It is a nonspecific term meaning 'this person is not functioning normally and we don't know what to do about it.' "

For twenty minutes I tried to gain a glimpse as to what troubled her. She answered evasively, obviously embar-rassed. Finally I narrowed it down to sex, by a kind of "twenty questions" process. She was obviously ashamed and reluctant to discuss it, but just as obviously wanted me

70

to dig it out of her. I covered most of the more obvious kinds of sexual problems, but drew a blank each time.

"Oh, you know," she said, looking at the ground.

A light dawned. "You mean masturbation?"

"Yes," she said miserably.

I was stunned. I had finally narrowed it down to an area involving nothing fundamentally wrong or sinful, but this poor woebegone young woman had labored for years under a glaring misconception. She thought she had done something so sinful that she could never be forgiven.

In the next few minutes I enlightened her. I told her God wasn't concerned about this matter one way or the other, and that nothing in the Bible condemned her.

For the first time she looked up at me. "Why has no one ever told me this?" she asked. "Human stupidity, I suppose. They didn't bother to ask the right questions, and you were too embarrassed to tell them."

She wrote me later to tell what a great load had been lifted. I groaned inwardly at the thought of a human being having been locked up in a mental institution and labeled "schizophrenic," who needed only to be led into an awareness of Christ's love, and told that she was all right.

When the Organism Malfunctions

When a business fails, or loses significant amounts of money, it is pretty evident that something is wrong with either the management, the product, or the economy. When any organization or organism begins to malfunction, it is an indication that something is wrong.

With the human organism, physical or emotional ills are simply external signals that "something is wrong." The "wrongness" may include anything from excessive fatigue, or blatant sin (violation of some cosmic law) to the corporate guilt of mankind, air pollution, or social injustice.

A deep, long-lasting depression, a phobia, an obsession, a physical pain, all are warnings of a "wrongness," a malfunction in an organism which was made to function perfectly. Every symptom, from a tension headache to cancer, points to a malfunction. Pain is simply a benevolent warning signal that something has gone wrong. The signal is there to alert us and encourage us to take appropriate action. Pain is therefore a blessing, as are all other symptoms, bidding us seek the source of the malfunction.

It has long been believed by authorities in the field of psychosomatic medicine that from fifty to eighty-five percent of physical ills stem from some emotional cause. In *The Natural Mind*, Andrew Weil, M.D., states:

> My experiences in allopathic medicine both as a patient and as a practitioner, have led me to conclude that all illness is psychosomatic. I do not use the word in the sense of "unreal" or "phony," as many allopaths do. Rather, I mean that all illness has both psychic and physical components, and it seems to me that the physical manifestations of illness (including the appearance of germs in tissues) are always effects, while the causes always lie within the realm of the mind, albeit the unconscious mind. In other words, the disease process seems to me to be initiated always by changes in consciousness. In the case of infectious illness, the initial causative change is not that germs appear to attack the body but that something happens in the person that permits a breakdown of the normal harmonious balance between the body and the microorganisms surrounding it.
>
> For example, the staphylococci that seem to cause boils are normal inhabitants of our skins. Most of the time, their relationship to us is symbiotic—mutually beneficial. Occasionally, that balance breaks down and boils appear. The problem is to restore the balance, not to make the staph germs disappear. An allopath, thinking that the germs cause the boils, treats this condition by trying to make the germs go away, by giving antibiotics. But antibiotics merely kill off the germs that are most inclined to form harmonious relationships with us, leaving behind the more aggressive, tougher ones that are less inclined to enter into balanced existence with their hosts. Over the past thirty years, allopathic hospitals have become virtual factories for turning out new strains of staph that are not only

highly resistant to several generations of antibiotics but also much more ruthless in their attacks on human beings.[1]

Weil's credentials are impressive. As a scientist employed by the federal government, he has conducted research projects of various kinds, in numerous medical fields. Whether or not he is correct in saying *all* illness is psychosomatic is not too important. It is sufficient to say that it is impossible to separate body, mind and emotions. They are one.

Illness and the Emotions

Dr. George Solomon of Stanford University has conducted an exhaustive survey into the relationship of emotional stress on cancer. He reports that under normal conditions the body's immunization system is able to keep us free of many diseases, but that emotional stress—especially sustained stress—can eventually overwhelm the immunity system, rendering us susceptible to numerous illnesses, including cancer.

Grief over the loss of a loved person or object may predispose one to malignancy, according to Dr. Lawrence LeShan of the Institute of Applied Biology, New York City. After spending more than six thousand hours with cancer patients he is of the opinion that unexpressed grief, or grief turned inward, seems to be a component in many cases of cancer. Among women of all ages who develop cancer, the greatest number is among widows.

A placid, delightful young minister on my church staff had what could be termed one of the world's worst cases of hay fever. It yielded to no known medication. He suffered uncomplainingly through several months each year.

I once told him, "Your emotions are tied up some way with your hay fever." Rather heatedly he asked why his emotions caused trouble only during the hay fever season. I told him I wasn't sure.

One day he entered my study and said, rather quietly,

that a contentious member was after him again. He was getting a little tired of it.

I said, "Look! That dear soul has been attacking you for years. Why don't you tell me how you *really* feel? I'm angry just hearing about it. In fact I'm hostile right now," I said, my voice rising. He got the message.

"O.K., I'm sick and tired of it. I'm going to do something about it!"

"Louder! You sound so pious it's sickening."

"I'll send her to the moon if she does it again," he shouted.

"Great! Now pound on the desk and tell me all about it."

He did, for five full minutes. It was honest and beautiful. Finally he stopped. "Hey! I can breathe through my nose for the first time in months! How about that?"

I encouraged him to continue being as tactful as necessary with people, but to come in and express his true feelings whenever he felt like it. He did so, frequently, with great benefit. Later he reported that about ninety-five percent of his symptoms had disappeared. Eventually he became able to express his "negative" feelings openly to people in a firm, nonhostile way. He no longer had to repress his true feelings and suffer the consequences.

God Does Not Will Sickness

Matthew writes that many followed Jesus, "and he healed them all." [2] But apparently Jesus did not heal *every* sick person without exception, for in Nazareth, we read that "he could do no mighty work there . . . because of their unbelief." [3] So even Jesus could not heal the unbelieving. Mark goes on to say, "Except that he laid his hands upon a few sick people and healed them."

But the willingness of Jesus to heal all who came *believing* tells us that pain and suffering are not the will of God. He does not will our suffering. It is not a part of God's plan. Jesus once referred to a woman who came to him for healing as "this woman . . . whom Satan bound for eighteen years." [4] It is Satan, not God, who is the source of sin, suffering and sorrow.

Physical and mental illness are the result of our own, or society's, failure at some point. I was having breakfast at a retreat with a group of people. A woman seated next to me told of a physical problem she was experiencing. A lump in her throat made swallowing difficult, and at times painful. A physician who examined her had reported that there was nothing wrong. "But there *is* something there that makes it hard for me to swallow," she said.

"What is it in your present life situation that you can't swallow?" I asked.

"Why, I have no idea."

We discussed it at some length, and finally I said, "I have a feeling that there is something in your life you can't accept, and probably something in the past that wants to come up and can't. We have half an hour before the first session," I added. "If you want to find the source of your problem let me know." I left the table. She resisted the idea, but two friends persuaded her to meet me in one of the private rooms. Time was short, so we worked rapidly, using a "healing of memories" technique. There are many ways to do this and each person seems to need a somewhat different approach. I had her pound a pillow.

In her case, though she was frightened, she went back quickly to age seven when a traumatic event occurred. She wept while three of us held her. Then we came to the present. I had her say, "I hate ———" as she pounded a pillow.

"I don't hate anything or anyone," she said.

"Pound! Say it!"

She tried, half-heartedly. I helped her pound. Finally she said, with tears of anger and frustration, "I *hate* the pressures being put on me by my family."

As she wept we held her again, until she was all cried out. Twenty-five minutes had elapsed, and I had to leave for the morning session. At noon she approached me, smiling: "The lump in my throat is gone. I'm ashamed of myself, but I keep swallowing to see if it's come back. It hasn't." I suppose it could if life's burdens become so great she can't "swallow" them.

Since she was an overly compliant person who had great difficulty in saying no to anyone, I told her, "Hereafter when asked to do something that you really can't handle, don't say no. Say, 'Yes, I'd be delighted to, but I just can't fit it into my schedule.'" This enabled her to avoid using the word *no,* something forbidden in her childhood.

Closely related to the healing of memories is "primal therapy," [5] a somewhat more complex and lengthy process involving daily or weekly sessions of one to two hours for weeks or months. In essence the primal approach holds that there is nothing wrong with any of us except childhood hurts, and that these hurts can be released only by reliving them—not just remembering them, which is a waste of time. In primal-type therapy we regress the subject to various ages of childhood, at which point the experience is relived, usually with a lot of pain and suffering. Either one relives it with this pain, or suffers the rest of his life—through psychosomatic pain, depression, or some form of neurosis. Though no one method applies to everyone, despite claims to the contrary, our experience with the use of primal-type therapy has been good in many instances. God works in many ways.

Prayer and Illness

A friend of mine, a delightful Christian physician, related an incident that intrigued me. A friend of his suffering from terminal cancer was experiencing almost unbearable pain. No form of medication had lessened his agony. He could not have visits with family and friends because of his excruciating pain. The physician asked seven friends to pray that the pain would let up. The next day the patient was free of pain for the first time in months. Now he could visit with his family as he longed to do. He died some time later with no further discomfort.

I do not have the faintest idea what spiritual laws were set in motion to relieve the pain of that man's last days on earth. But I am convinced that it was not a "miracle," in the sense of violating natural law. Rather I believe that prayer invokes a higher law, just as a B-47 flies, not by violating the law of gravity, but by having been designed to work in harmony with the laws of aerodynamics. Jesus healed, I feel confident, by invoking laws and principles higher than the law of disease and death. They were not miracles, if by miracles one means a violation of natural law.

Love may be a lifesaver, Dr. John C. Cassel believes. Addressing the Congress on Environmental Health sponsored by the AMA, Cassel said prevention of disease depends as much on a person's psychological and social climate as it does on such things as diet and housing. Some doctors don't believe there is such a thing as generalized susceptibility to disease. But if there isn't, he said, it would be hard to "explain why divorced men have a death rate three to five times higher than married men of the same age."

Three state mental hospitals received 140 patients in a given period of time:

—10% could not name a church or pastor;

—only 20% were active church members;

—the balance were nonchurch members, or fringe members.

There appears to be some correlation between mental health and active participation in the life of a church. This being so, it suggests that God wills wholeness of mind, body and circumstances, and that fellowship with God and his people help provide that wholeness.

Jesus did not say, "Father, *if it be Thy will*, restore sight to this blind man." He touched and healed the blind. He "saw" the sick and maimed as "well," "whole," complete in mind and body.

When you pray for someone, or yourself, envision that person as whole, the way God wants him. If there is a circumstance that is not right, "see" it as right. Phrases such as "if it be thy will," or "not my will but thine" have a place, but too often they are a cop-out. Remember that only once did Jesus use that phrase, and never as applying to someone whom he healed.

Jean was five or six years old when her mother was sent away to a mental institution. She overheard a neighbor say, "I hope Jean doesn't inherit her mother's insanity." From then on she lived a life of fear, wondering when she would succumb to the supposed hereditary weakness. In a college class a teacher said (as Jean heard it) that "insanity can be inherited." Jean leaped to her feet and screamed, "That's not so!" Then she sank back into her seat, horribly embarrassed by the spectacle she had made of herself.

She lived on under the threat of going insane, until one day she heard a minister say, "We do not inherit the limitations of our parents, but the potential of our heavenly Father." That one sentence changed her entire life, and her concept of herself. She became a new person, unafraid, glowing with assurance. She knew the truth at last. Subsequently she became an ordained minister so that she could help spread the good news that had changed her life.

"Men commonly deplore some lesser sin in order to avoid confronting some greater sin they prefer not to face."

GABRIEL MONTELBAN

7.
Guilt, Forgiveness, and Prayer

HAZEL, A FRIEND OF MINE in her late sixties, was on her way to Taiwan, enjoying the luxury liner which visited various ports en route. A strong wind arose, and the ship began to roll. Someone spread the rumor that a typhoon was expected.

Hazel began to experience sheer panic out of all proportion to the actual danger. Suddenly she became aware of a long-buried memory. Sixty years before she and her two sisters had been out on a lake in a small rowboat. Hazel tipped the boat and it capsized, throwing the three occupants into the water. There was imminent danger of drowning, but the girls were rescued.

An older sister, presumably in charge, was blamed, and Hazel let her assume the full responsibility despite terrible guilt feelings. As the great liner rolled in the giant waves, Hazel dealt with that long-buried memory. She could see the reason for her overreaction. Unresolved guilt and consequent fear of punishment had lain dormant for more than fifty years.

Time does not diminish guilt. An event may be in the distant past, but the memory with any attendant guilt is in the present. Guilt requires confession, followed by forgiveness, or it demands punishment in some form. It is not God who requires this, but an inexorable inner judicial system.

Guilt—the Violation of Our Integrity

One price we pay for being human is the experience of shame and guilt. The two are not the same. Shame may produce embarrassment, constriction of the throat, a knot in the stomach, flushing, and an accelerated heartbeat. It is the very unpleasant realization that we have fallen in our own estimation and in the estimation of others. It may not be so much that the act was wrong, as that it reveals us to others as "wrong," "faulty," "inadequate." Pride is at the root of shame.

Pride is not simply thinking well of ourselves, but insisting that others think well of us. When we "blow it" and reveal our less-than-ideal selves to others, the result is shame. Our image is tarnished. One who is prone to shame has something to hide. Hence he must always censor what he says or does.

Guilt is something different, in that it is a violation of one's integrity. One of the greatest temptations I ever experienced occurred when I was about eight or nine years old. The little church our family attended in a tiny Texas town was conducting an "ice cream social." It was a combination fund-raising and social event. The women brought home-made ice cream and sold it for ten cents a dish. The event was held on the church lawn. A man I knew passed by and asked what was going on. I told him. He handed me a dollar (a vast sum to me) and said, "Here, buy some ice cream for all your friends." Temptation hit hard! I clutched a whole dollar in my hand and thought, "I could buy ten dishes of ice cream for myself and no one would ever know. Besides," I rationalized, "the money all goes to help the church no matter who eats the ice cream."

But the inner self never accepts a rationalization. I had heard the man say clearly, "Buy some ice cream for *all your friends.*" This may seem like a trivial incident, but violating one's integrity is never a minor thing. I struggled with the temptation, and even felt guilty over the fact that I had permitted the temptation to arise. Finally virtue triumphed. I found nine friends and treated them each to ice cream. A second temptation then presented itself: "Perhaps I can take credit for being generous, and can play the role of the big spender." Finally I was able to discard this. But it was no easy struggle.

I have battled hundreds—thousands—of temptations since, and lost many of them, but that one stands out. I didn't succumb. I maintained my integrity, but I felt very guilty about even entertaining such thoughts. I didn't know then that temptation is not sin.

Bad Parents, Bad Religion, and Bad Sex

The head of a large mental institution once said, "Most of these people are here because of either bad parents, bad religion, or bad sex." It could be said with equal validity that most of the difficulties encountered by those of us outside the walls of a mental institution stem from the same source to a lesser degree.

Everyone from Adam and Eve until now has been reared by parents who were in some degree faulty individuals. Original sin has been passed down to us through faulty environment, and conceivably genetically through faulty genes.

Bad religion, to use the term of the hospital director, could include an ultrastrict, moralistic, judgmental type of religious training. The God of my childhood was very angry and judgmental. Jesus loved children, but God was writing all of my misdeeds in a big book. It was this God, not Jesus, who was going to judge me.

There are many other variations of "bad religion," but perhaps the worst of the lot is the type of religion that is life-denying, joyless, grim, and preoccupied with attempts to avoid the wrath of a just but angry God.

"Bad sex" of course has to do with misuse of, or misinformation concerning the love-sex drive, one of the most powerful of the God-given impulses. Masters and Johnson, who have conducted exhaustive research in this field, report that in at least half of all marriages sex relations are a disaster. Somewhere our society—religion, schools, family—took the wrong fork in the road. Once there were things people couldn't talk about. Now they can't talk about anything else; and either extreme is neurotic.

Mary Anne attended a series of Saturday workshops conducted regularly at the Yokefellow Center in Burlingame, California. About thirty persons were present at the one where she gained sufficient courage to tell—for the first time—the story of an event that had marred her life.

She was about fourteen or fifteen when her father's best friend was asked to drive her to their new home in another part of the state. The friend, however, struck with Mary Anne's youthful beauty, took her on a terrifying, week-long tour of motels throughout the state. The kidnapped girl was raped repeatedly.

When finally she was rescued, her mother's first words were, "Think of the shame you've brought on our family." The father made no serious effort to prosecute the kidnapper.

Mary Anne, now a poised, cultured woman of fifty, relived the terror of that week and shared it for the first time. She was almost overwhelmed by the wave of understanding and compassion which engulfed her. A man sitting near me was in tears. He went and sat at her feet. Holding her hands, and with tears streaming down his face, he told her that he could understand. His sister, he said, had been raped, killed, and her body thrown on the city garbage dump.

Mary Anne had been made to feel vaguely guilty, wrong, evil. Her mother's words still haunted her. Never having shared the traumatic event previously, she still felt the little girl-rejection and condemnation of her mother, and the relative indifference of her father.

Mary Anne's bewildered, hurt, inner child of the past was held lovingly by the group. In two or three successive sessions, as she dealt with ancient feelings of being "guilty" and "bad," she finally came to feel what she knew in her head—that it was false guilt, not real guilt.

Many persons suffer untold anguish over false guilt relating to sex. Some end up in mental institutions. Others live out lives of quiet desperation and remorse.

But there is real guilt in this area, too, for uncounted millions have violated their integrity, not so much by intent as through human weakness. Jesus understood the problem, and thus was able to say to one guilty woman, "Neither do I condemn you; go, and do not sin again" [1]—or rephrased, "I do not condemn you. You may go now, but don't keep this up or you will harm yourself."

Journey to the Alabaster City

At a one-day workshop I asked the participants to join me in a fantasy. A fantasy is "real," in that the imagined experiences are subjectively real, a kind of waking dream. I said, "Close your eyes and imagine that you have experienced a painless death and suddenly find yourself standing outside the gates of heaven. Some distance away the Alabaster City gleams in the light whose source is Christ. He is seated at the center of the city at a fountain. He awaits you. He has all the time in eternity.

"You will see approaching you various people from the past and present. In each case there is or has been an impaired relationship. Before you will feel free to enter the City you will experience a need to clear up any such impaired relationships." Some taped stereo music then started them on their journey to heaven.

Twenty minutes later as they "came back," they related their experiences. One in particular intrigued me. A young woman said, "Suddenly I was there. I could see the Alabaster City in the distance. My stepfather (a sadistic, half-insane man) and my mother (an unloving religious fanatic) appeared. Then my ex-husband (as sadistic as my stepfather) joined us.

"I saw that they were covered with bleeding, gaping

wounds, and looking down, I discovered that I, too, bled from many cuts and gashes. With no explanations (it seemed that none was needed), we put our arms around each other and walked into the center of the City. Jesus was there at the fountain. He seemed to be more thoroughly mild and approachable than the most loving of my friends. He put his arms around each of us, and in the warmth of his total acceptance and love, our wounds slowly began to disappear."

To me, the beauty of her fantasy lay in the awareness that sadistic and unloving people and religious fanatics are, like the rest of us, all "wounded," damaged by life and circumstances. She saw, too, despite a judgmental, religious background, that Christ healed and forgave instantly, in love, and did not judge or condemn.

What Is Sin?

A Yokefellow group member, a bus driver, told how he had been tempted into a temporary loss of his integrity.

"Other drivers no better than I were being paid more than I was getting. I asked for a raise and was refused. I knew I deserved a raise, so I did what ninety percent of the other drivers were doing. I began to take out of the cash receipts about as much as I thought I deserved. But I couldn't live with myself. Besides I kept waiting for the police. I thought the supervisor looked at me suspiciously. I felt guilty, because I was. So I quit stealing. Two days of that was all I could stand." He could not endure the loss of integrity.

God does not refuse to hear our prayers because we are guilty, but the biblical principle holds: "If our hearts do not condemn us, we have confidence before God." [2] When we feel self-condemned we *don't* approach God boldly, in confidence and in faith.

Sin is whatever clouds our consciousness. It is whatever makes it harder to pray, or makes it more difficult to appreciate beauty and truth.

Sin is anything that impairs a relationship and leaves it in that condition.

Sin is whatever makes us less compassionate.

It is anything that mars our relationship with God, limits our relationship with others, or causes us to like ourself less.

Sin is any attitude that prevents us from following the light and acting upon insights we know are true and valid.

Sin, then, is a wrong against God, others, or self. It is anything which blocks our growth or that of our neighbor.

Virtually any action or attitude can be rationalized, *but the unconscious mind never accepts a rationalization.* It knows the truth. Intellectualizing and rationalizing can be a way of hiding behind the verbiage, as Adam hid behind the foliage.

A letter received from a friend some time ago illustrates the crafty nature of the rationalizing self:

> I am recognizing and dealing with the fact that my lack of physical stamina, and chronic fatigue, are the result of repressing my emotions. It's painful for me to learn about myself—my unconscious self. I am always shocked to find out what I'm like. I thought I was the very opposite of what I really am! I thought I was pretty great. Instead I was prim and proper and unreachable, and pious as hell, plus superior and self-righteous. Now I know I'm a sinner like everyone else. And the great news is that it's okay to be a sinner. That's what Jesus and His cross are all about, the acceptance of sinners like me. Hallelujah!

How to Forgive Yourself

Now we are ready to consider a formula for achieving self-forgiveness:

Here is a list of opposites.

sacred - secular	perfect - imperfect
holy - unholy	pure - impure
good - bad	loving - unloving
right - wrong	saint - sinner
strong - weak	worthy - unworthy
true - false	righteous - evil
honest - dishonest	generous - selfish

The list could be extended indefinitely, with many other

opposites. What we are dealing with here is the conflict between "good" and "bad," "right" and "wrong," "black" and "white"—a murderous dichotomy.

I recommend the following formula which I have used with profit. Choose your own list of four or five of the above opposites. Then make your prayer of affirmation like this:

Lord, I am neither good nor bad. I am both, and you accept me, love me and forgive me.

I am neither right nor wrong. I am both, and you accept me, love me and forgive me.

I am neither pure nor impure. I am both, and you accept me, love me and forgive me.

I am neither worthy nor unworthy. I am both, and you accept me, love me and forgive me.

I am neither generous nor selfish. I am both, and you accept me, love me and forgive me. I now forgive myself.

Stop trying to be "good!" You will never make it. Instead try to let the Spirit of Christ permeate your life. Pray this prayer of affirmation, or something similar, in order to overcome the "good-bad" conflict. Do it daily, regularly. Instead of trying to be "good," or "righteous," try to be *his*, and to live in intimate fellowship with him.

You may fail often, as I have. But the glory of Christ's redeeming love is that he accepts us back into fellowship though we fall a thousand times.

8.
The Fear of God
Can Be the Beginning of Neurosis

A MINISTER REFERRED Rochelle to me for counseling. She
was middle-aged, divorced, and held a responsible position
with a large firm.

Rochelle was deeply depressed and strongly paranoid. She
was convinced that the members of her church all disliked
her, and that everyone at work avoided her for some unknown reason. She insisted that people riding on the bus
would consistently avoid sitting beside her. The whole world
was filled with people conspiring against her, and she was
certain that her immediate superior had it in for her. There
was more, but this was enough to indicate that Rochelle was
a full-blown paranoiac. How she was able to hold down her
job was a mystery to me.

Paranoia can be roughly defined as excessive suspicion,
often involving a severe persecution complex. It takes many
forms, and stems from numerous sources. One common
source is alternating love and rejection in childhood; or a
home atmosphere lacking in love, where punishment is severe.

I asked Rochelle about her early childhood. She said, "I
loved and feared my father. He would offer affection, but
when he got angry over something I'd done that displeased
him, he'd become livid with rage. Then he'd make me sit on

a stool for hours, silent and motionless. If I went to sleep and fell off the stool he'd put me back on it. If I moved a muscle he'd whip me. When I upset my milk at breakfast he'd slam me onto the stool, and when he'd have to leave for work, he'd tell my mother not to let me move for another two hours. Usually she'd let me go as soon as he'd leave the house."

That was just one of many refined tortures he dreamed up. There were many others. She lived in constant terror that she might do something that would arouse his wrath.

"Tell me how you feel about God," I asked.

"Oh, God's angry with me, too, I'm sure. I don't know what I've done to displease him, but I must have done something, or these terrible things wouldn't be happening to me now."

It is worse than useless to try to explain reality to a person with a persecution complex. So after a number of counseling sessions I put Rochelle in a Yokefellow group where she could learn to experience some of the love and acceptance she had never known as a child, or even in her brief marriage. Timidly at first, then with growing courage, she began to accept our love. We became her family. Her paranoia gradually diminished.

Rochelle felt toward God what she had felt toward her father: mingled love and fear. To try to tell her what God was like would have been futile. An hour's dissertation on the love of God could not wipe out the feelings of a lifetime. But she came gradually to experience the love of God as it was transmitted by persons who cared about her and reached out to her in love. I told her never to refer to God as "Father," and to pray to Jesus. "God, the Father" will always have negative connotations for Rochelle.

God Can Seem Like Your Human Father

There are exceptions, but in general it can be said that at a *feeling* level God is like one's human father. Various factors may modify or intensify this. A strong, warm, accepting mother can often lessen the influence of a rejecting, punishing father; or, some other loving male figure—uncle, grandfather, or neighbor—may help a child gain a more realistic concept of God.

I observed this in the case of a delightful young man who came to see me. He wanted to know how he could help his father. I had met and counseled briefly with the father, a highly successful man who was cold, austere, and rigid. The son was deeply concerned about his father. I asked if he could shed any light on his father's early life. He told me of two incidents.

One Christmas Eve, when the father was about five or six, there was a tremendous explosion in the house. The little boy ran out into the yard. His father followed him calmly and said, "Son, I just shot Santa Claus." That was the sadistic manner he chose to let his son know that "there isn't any Santa Claus."

But there were presents just the same. His most treasured gift was a watch. On Christmas Day the father took his son out into the backyard and hung his own gold watch on the fence. Then next to it he hung his young son's new watch. Handing the boy a .22 rifle he said, "See if you can hit my watch." Never having fired a gun before, of course he missed. The father then took careful aim and smashed his son's new Christmas watch into a thousand pieces.

When the young man related this I said, "Your dad had a sadistic father, didn't he?"

"Insane, I'd say. No emotion was ever permitted in the home, either anger, joy or sorrow, and of course, no love or affection."

That one incident, of course, was only one of many.

I asked the young man how it happened that he had become an earnest Christian. He said, "I identified with my mother who more than made up for my father's coldness and rejection."

"Well, if you'd like to help your father," I said, "for one thing don't send him any tracts, or write him letters urging him to change. Just pray for him. And," I added, "while you are praying remember that your dad, in God's sight, may be doing pretty well, all things considered."

"How's that?" He looked genuinely confused.

"You know the statement of Jesus, 'Every one to whom much is given, of him will much be required.' [1] Now state the converse of that."

He said, "Well I guess it would be 'Unto whom little is given, little will be required.' "

"Right. So love your father, pray for him, and wait for the miracle of God's grace to work in some way that you and I cannot even imagine."

He rose to leave, smiled, and said, "I feel greatly relieved. Thanks!"

Considering what his father was like, I was surprised at the young man's charming, open, loving personality. The influence of a warm, loving Christian mother had been sufficient to overcome the negative effect of a cold, rejecting father.

An Absentee Father Can Make a "Distant God"

Sally, married and the mother of three grown children, announced firmly that she was an agnostic. From time to time she would refer to herself as an atheist rather than an agnostic. Quite often, however, she used the phrase, "As God is my witness. . . ." I asked her why she called on God to witness her veracity when she alternately doubted or denied his existence.

"Oh, it's just an expression," she laughed, "but sometimes I'm not too sure about God, one way or the other."

Her father, as she described him, was undemonstrative, entirely lacking in warmth, and was away from home most of the time.

"So," I said, "an absentee father equals an absentee or nonexistent God."

"Oh, I don't buy all that psychological garbage. When someone can convince me there is a God, then I'll believe."

But, in general, an absentee father can mean an absentee God, and a hostile, punitive father can leave a child with a feeling that God is angry and judgmental. Long after I knew intellectually that "God is love," at a feeling level I experienced the same fear of God that I felt toward my father. Intellectually I conceived of God as being like Jesus. Emotionally I felt he was the Old Testament God—stern, demanding, and ready to vent his wrath upon all who sinned. The influence of a loving mother was not enough to eradicate the combined influences of a just-but-stern father, coupled with a vast deal of hellfire evangelistic preaching.

Julia, thirty-four, happily married and the mother of three lovely children, shared with her Yokefellow group the feelings she had about God.

"He's distant, remote, and rather unapproachable. He's too busy and preoccupied to hear me when I pray. Oh, of course, I know in my head that he isn't like that, but at a feeling level he's just exactly like my father. He was an evangelist, away from home most of the time. When he was home, he was either tired or studying. I sensed that he was a wonderful person—but he was sort of 'for other people,' too busy to pay any attention to me. God feels the same way, so I never repeat the Lord's prayer. I just pray to Jesus. He's warm and loving and accepting. I get along fine with him."

It is highly probable, in the opinion of many psychiatrists and psychologists, that no one ever was committed to a mental institution who had experienced genuine love from both parents in childhood, in a form the child could accept.

A woman once told me of having been abandoned by her father, badly mistreated by her mother, and sexually molested repeatedly by relatives and friends of the family. No one else in the family attended church, but something drew her to a nearby church. There, for the first time, she learned about love. "I knew that at least God loved me, and the people at the church loved me. No one else did, but I lived on the love I got at church."

Eventually she married a man much older than she, in an unconscious effort to find the father she scarcely remembered.

Despite the tragedies and scars of childhood, she had become a delightful person. Yet, her voice and manner carried a note of sadness that I felt sure was a permanent part of her personality.

What Is God Like?

Early childhood conditioning is important, but it is not *everything*. Despite what life has done to us, we are still free to choose, to continue our growth, to become more open to the Spirit of God—the God of love, and joy and laughter, who never gives up his relentless search for us when we wander.

Just what is God like?

Certainly he is not the tribal God perceived by a primitive group of Hebrews, who thought he wanted them to slaughter all of the inhabitants of the towns and cities they encountered in Palestine. Their idea of a storm God on Mt. Sinai, whose essence they carried with them in the ark, grew gradually to the point where some of their prophets denounced animal sacrifices. Eventually Micah asked rhetorically, "What does the Lord require of you but to do justice, and to love kindness, and to walk humbly with your God?" [2]

And finally there was the supreme revelation of God, One who dared to say, "He who has seen me has seen the Father"; [3] "I and the Father are one." [4]

Jesus did not urge us to fear God, but to love him—to love him supremely, above all else. I could not love a God whom I feared. I fear the consequences of disobeying the benevolent, cosmic principles governing his universe, but I love the Creator, the Source of all Life.

If the fear of God can be the beginning of neurosis—or at least a warped personality—then the love of God can be the beginning of wholeness.

Get Your Priorities in Order

Jesus saw the people of his day—then as now—tense with anxiety about food, clothing, shelter, the future. To them he said, in effect, "No, you are going at it backwards. Your priorities are all wrong. The very first thing you must do is to seek to enter the kingdom of God. This involves accepting new principles and priorities. This spiritual kingdom is one wherein you are to love God, and seek his wonderful purpose in your life. When you do this, all the other things you are so concerned about will come to you as a matter of course. You are making material things your primary goal. You must make spiritual growth your chief aim in life, and material things will follow." [5]

Then he stated some of the principles governing this spiritual kingdom. They involved love for God, for one's fellow man, and a proper love for oneself.[6] Another principle concerned loving one's enemy.[7] An enemy is anyone who regards you with enmity, or with whom you have an impaired relationship.

Another basic principle of this spiritual kingdom (or mental and spiritual state of mind) had to do with giving: "Give, and it will be given to you . . . " [8]

Still another of his teachings had to do with forgiveness. Simon Peter did not fully understand this principle, and asked, "Lord, how often shall my brother sin against me, and I forgive him? As many as seven times?" Perhaps Peter expected to be praised for this generous estimate. But Jesus told him, "I do not say to you seven times, but seventy times seven." [9] In other words, "Forgive without limit, as God forgives you unconditionally and limitlessly."

So, to love, to give and to forgive; to deal with the evil and unworthy just as God deals with us in our worst moments— this seems to be the fundamental condition for entering the spiritual kingdom, the new state of consciousness, where God can reach us, and give us the desires of our hearts.

9.
Answered
and Unanswered Prayer

NAOMI CONSULTED with me about her husband, a confirmed alcoholic. In the course of our counseling sessions she came gradually to see that she had married a passive, dependent man with sadistic tendencies, in an unconscious effort to re-create and resolve the relationship with her sadistic father. She also discovered that she was quite masochistic—consciously hating the abuse she received at the hands of her husband when he was drinking, but unconsciously needing it in order to suffer. Masochism could be defined loosely as the "pleasure through pain" principle. It is, of course, an unconscious need.

Through counseling and participation in a small group, Naomi gained enough self-respect and courage so that she could say, "I don't know whether my prayers will be answered or not. I am not sure that I can stay with Bob indefinitely. But I am going to straighten out my own attitudes, and become strong enough to live with him if I feel I should, or courageous enough to leave him if I find I must."

Naomi's growth continued. She refused to tolerate violence when Bob had been drinking, and simply left the house when he became abusive. On occasion she spent the night away from home until he sobered up. She became a regular attendant at church, participated in a Yokefellow sharing group, and managed to grow emotionally and spiritually. She grew beyond resentment and martyrdom. After six or eight years, when it was quite evident that her husband had no intention of seeking help, and no desire whatever to change, she left him. A year or two later she met and married a man with whom she has been quite happy.

God Cannot, in Love, Answer Every Prayer

Naomi had prayed earnestly during the entire time. Her prayers initially had been, "O Lord, help my husband to see the importance of attending AA meetings regularly." Later she changed her prayer. She asked to be shown if there was anything in her which might be aggravating the situation. She prayed for God's perfect will for Bob, for serenity of spirit, and the power to face whatever came. In the process she became a very poised individual, with quiet inner strength.

Her original prayer could not be answered under the circumstances. Her husband, a free moral agent, had the power to resist even God. But her prayer for strength and serenity in the face of adversity was answered, and she was enabled to live without bitterness.

Naomi implemented her prayer. She not only attended church regularly and participated in sharing groups so that she could look within and gain spiritual strength, but she also attended weekly meetings of Alanon, the arm of Alcoholics Anonymous which helps relatives of alcoholics learn how to live with the problems they encounter.

Obviously not every prayer can be answered in the affirmative by God. Some of our prayers are so short-sighted and limited that God would be doing us a great disservice if he were to grant every petition.

Monica, the mother of Augustine, was a devout Christian living on the north coast of Africa. Her restless, brilliant son announced his intention of going to Rome, then the center of every conceivable form of licentiousness. Monica prayed earnestly that he would not go, but the headstrong young Augustine packed up and went to Rome. Her specific prayer had not been answered.

But in Rome, seemingly by accident, Augustine came under the influence of one of the most remarkable bishops of the early Church. As a result Augustine became a Christian and ultimately one of the most outstanding Christian leaders of his day. His writings are still studied.

Monica's specific petition went unanswered, but her larger prayer for her son's ultimate welfare was granted.

Two Spiritual Laws

After her first skiing lesson a young woman said, "I never knew that the law of gravity was so strictly enforced." There are spiritual laws governing prayer which are just as inexorable as the law of gravity. There are many such laws, or principles, but two are most important.

1. *Intensity of Desire*

The half-hearted prayer is basically just God-oriented wishful thinking. What you seek or desire with all your heart is your true prayer, whether it is "uttered or unexpressed." Unless the desire is deep and earnest, spiritual forces are diffused. It is not that God requires intensity of desire in order to grant our petitions, but that we are rendered ineligible until we sort out our many scattered desires, and focus upon the ones which are paramount. Half-hearted and intensive prayers differ as much as a shotgun and a rifle. A shotgun fires a scattering of small shot. A rifle focuses the same explosive energy behind one single bullet and fires it vastly farther, and with greater effect.

The diffused, scattered prayer is on the order of little Linus's ambition. He expressed the desire to be a humble, wealthy, highly successful country doctor. Then he added, "with a red sports car."

2. *Continuity.*

Our psychic forces are diffused and adulterated by the very fact of living in a temporal world, of making a living, rearing a family, coping with life's everyday problems. The earnest desire needs to be kept at the forefront of one's attention. Our "quick results" civilization, with instant coffee, TV dinners, and fast worldwide telephone dialing, renders us impatient. Having to drive behind a slow-moving vehicle for sixty seconds is enough to make most drivers grossly impatient.

Intensity, continuity and patience are required: intensity so that our spiritual forces will not be diffused and scattered; continuity and patience so that we will not abandon the desire until we have received an answer. The response may come in strange ways.

Monica did not receive specifically what she sought, but a much greater blessing was granted her as she patiently prayed day after day for the greatest desire of her heart: her son's welfare.

I once counseled with a young woman whose parents were alcoholics. Most of their friends were either alcoholics or heavy drinkers. How many hundreds of times she prayed and longed for the love they were incapable of giving. She was in her twenties before she found people who could love her, and in whose love she could believe. She never gave up! And what a loving, charming, happy person she became. Though the answer was long delayed, her patience and determination were rewarded.

It was not reluctance on the part of God which prevented her from receiving love sooner. God has granted humans the power to thwart his purposes. Her parents were unwilling or unable to respond to the spirit of God. But the daughter's patient, determined search for love ultimately found fulfillment.

Delayed Answers to Prayer

Whenever I have prayed about something, and an affirmative answer has not been forthcoming, I sense that the problem is usually within me. When the answer is delayed, I may discover that there is something wrong with my attitude, or I have prayed half-heartedly, or lacked patience.

Often I have prayed for the wrong thing, and have been shown my error by subsequent events.

A young married woman made a profession of faith years ago, and I baptized her. Her husband, Wilford, a belligerent agnostic, was indignant and very hostile over her decision to unite with the church. I called in the home one evening soon after she had made her decision. Her husband came to the door. "Oh, it's you," he said rather ungraciously.

"Yes, I decided to drop in for a cup of coffee."

It's a bit difficult to be hostile toward a guest in your home, drinking coffee, but he managed. It was a rather tense visit, but he warmed up somewhat during the evening. The following week his wife and I entered into a pact. We agreed that we would pray for God's perfect will for her husband. I urged her not to specify what that might be, since the temptation is strong to pray for someone else to change so that life may be easier for us.

We kept to our agreement for nine long years. During this time Wilford began to attend church quite regularly, though he refused to participate in any activities. One evening I sat down with a book at home, grateful for the first night in weeks that I could stay home. I no sooner began to read, than the name "Wilford" began to intrude into my consciousness. I tried several times to resume my reading, but the name kept coming to mind.

I went to the phone and called him. "Wilford, I'd like to drop in and visit you for a few minutes."

"Oh? Well, we were just going bowling, but I suppose we could wait." Ten minutes later I was seated in their home. I made it brief:

"Wilford, you've been attending church regularly for some time. I'm delighted that you do. But I had a strong feeling tonight that there is another step which you may be prepared to take. I felt that you were ready to be baptized and unite with the church."

He looked thoughtful, then said, "Yes, I hadn't really

thought about it consciously, but I really think I ought to. I believe I'm ready."

Wilford became a loyal member, and served his church with deep devotion.

Nine years is a long time to wait. My impatient "inner child" much prefers quicker results. But if God could wait forty years for the children of Israel to have a change of heart, I can manage to restrain my impatience and take the long view.

"My God, My God, Why . . . ?"

It is somewhat more difficult to understand the prayer to which no affirmative answer is ever given: the husband who prays for the recovery of his wife, who dies; the parents who pray fervently that a sick child will be spared; the illness endured without relief; the errant son or daughter who rejects all overtures of love. Experiences such as these prompt one to cry, with Job, "Why dost thou hide thy face . . . ?"[1]

Yet, it was the same despairing Job who proclaimed, when the vision was clearer, "I know that my redeemer lives"![2]

Jesus cried out on the Cross, "My God, my God, why . . . ?"[3] There was no immediate response; but the answer became clear on that first resurrection morning.

The Apostle Paul's plea, three times repeated, that his "thorn in the flesh" might be removed was never granted, but he was reassured by an inner voice which said, "My grace is all you need; power comes to its full strength in weakness."[4]

It has been said that "man seeks a better plan; God desires a better man." Put another way, there is something within most of us which would eagerly seize some magical formula, a quick and easy technique for getting our needs met instantly. The world is full of people searching for the one simple answer. Hope is held out that perhaps astrology, or transcendental meditation, or a new guru, alpha waves, or some new charismatic religious leader may provide the simple answer.

Some of these may help. But the longer I live the more I am willing to come to terms with the inexorable fact that trees and human beings grow slowly. The tragically slow spiritual growth of the twelve whom Jesus chose gives me solace. Even after the descent of the Holy Spirit, when they were given new power, there were many personality problems to be resolved. The Apostle Paul, Christ's most valuable emissary, endured unimaginable hardships and disappointments. The way was not made easy for him simply because he was a spiritual giant. Though he had been granted a vision of "the third heaven" he was not spared illness, shipwreck, beatings, persecution, and imprisonment.[5]

The innate childhood love of magic dies slowly, if ever. How reluctantly we gave up our belief in Santa Claus, in fairies, in a life where everything ends happily.

We live in a world where a Christ can be crucified, his disciples put to the sword, banished or imprisoned. Jesus actually promised his followers that "in the world you will have trouble. But courage! The victory is mine; I have conquered the world." [6]

Though we humans search for lasting peace and prosperity, and a life without suffering, we can be assured that life on this planet will be fraught with some difficulties, if not tragedies. There is no guarantee that we will be spared suffering.

God Wills Our Growth

Then, of what value is prayer, if it does not provide an alternative to disaster, guidance for decisions, and some assurance that God is interested in our welfare?

When my son and daughter moved away from home to start life on their own, there were times when I wanted desperately to rush in and help them financially and otherwise. Each had minor financial problems, as they learned how to handle their limited resources in a society where every television show urges us to buy, buy, buy. I let them know that if disaster ever struck, I stood ready to help. But more than they needed any financial help I could give them, they needed to learn how to live on their incomes. The discipline of saving for some long-desired item is an essential part of growing up, of maturing.

God could grant our every wish, and make life infinitely easier, but in love he refuses to do so. For the farmer he provides the resources: soil, sun, fertility, moisture. The farmer must plow, harrow, plant, cultivate, harvest. An agriculture expert estimated that God does roughly 90 percent of the work, the farmer 10.

The same thing holds true in other areas of life. The resources are here. God will not do it all for us, or we would be forever crippled emotionally and spiritually.

When our son was tiny I sat feeding him one evening, spoonful by spoonful, half of the food dropping on me or the floor. Suddenly he turned and looked at me, as though some great thought was formulating in his mind. Then he looked at the spoon in my hand. He seized it, plunged it into the bowl and stabbed at his mouth. He missed it the first time or two, but finally found it. It was very messy for the next few minutes, but what a look of achievement lit up his face as he finally dropped the spoon back into the bowl. He had done it by himself!

The Father watches over us, I am confident, longing for us to grow, to become mature, to expand and develop our mental, emotional, and spiritual powers. He offers us all the resources of our physical world. Spiritual guidance and power are available, but we must get quiet and receptive in order to receive them. He is willing for us to try and fail, to explore, experiment, to learn by trial and error. Added to our human best there is available the power of the Holy Spirit. He will not force or coerce us. But he is there, in the person of one who said, "I am with you always to the close of the age." [7]

Growth in Groups

In his remarkable book, *Prayer Can Change Your Life,*[8]
Dr. William Parker, a psychologist formerly associated with
the University of Redlands, points out that it is impossible
to surrender to God or deal with portions of the personality
which are unknown to us. It was he who pioneered the use of
psychological tests as a spiritual growth device. Yokefellows, Inc., has since expanded this concept. Some sixty thousand persons have used the spiritual growth inventories
provided by Yokefellows, in groups of eight to twelve persons.

A pastor, participating in his first group, wrote: "This is
the greatest thing I've found. What we accomplish in the
group experience is thrilling as compared to the old-fash-
ioned prayer meeting, where we just went through the mo-
tions. The groups in our church have been non-judgmental,
non-moralistic. I shall never cease to be grateful. You people
have found something. Some of my members have said,
'Pastor, you're a changed man.' It is my release, in being
able now to relate to people. I love them more sincerely; in-
hibitions are down. I see the New Testament and the teachings of Jesus in a totally new light. I have always known
these things somewhere in the back of my mind, but now
they are operative. I am a better counselor, less judgmental,
more insightful, and far more effective."

A member of another group wrote, "I have at last found
peace in prayer and meditation as the result of my group experience. I am learning to understand and accept myself.
Never before had I understood what was wrong with my
life. I have two neurotic daughters, and a mother who demanded so much of my time that I couldn't give attention to
my own family. I have become calmer, and now realize that
my early environment was responsible for my inner conflicts."

My own experience in a Yokefellow group parallels the
discoveries of thousands of group participants. For many

years I had experienced a vague, all-pervasive inner tension. Having had it most or all of my life I could not have been aware of what it would be like to be without it. The tension produced a number of physical symptoms, none very serious, but still aggravating. I could pray about the tension, and try to relax, but I was not able to resolve the problem. Finally, as the result of my Yokefellow experience, and one of the spiritual growth inventories, I began to discover what should have been obvious all along. I was suffering from a mild floating anxiety. That put a label on it, but did not cure it. What was the anxiety all about? Where did it originate? There was nothing in my current life situation to account for it.

Eventually, by remaining faithful to the daily quiet time, I was able to dredge up the source of the anxiety, and then deal with it. Floating anxiety originates in some nebulous fear, usually of long standing. But what was I afraid of? What had I feared all of my life?

In a moment of complete quiet and utter relaxation the answer floated into consciousness: *Fear of judgment*. As the words formed themselves in my mind, I could see my father's face, tense, anxious, and to me, judgmental. I could not know then that his perpetual frown stemmed largely from personal worries. I sensed that I had caught his anxiety partly by osmosis, and partly through fear of his criticism. And in the same flash of intuition I saw the faces of scores of evangelists who had pounded hellfire judgment into my young mind. It rang all sorts of bells. I had found the source of my life-long tension at last, and now I knew what to pray about. It was clear that praying about tension and anxiety was useless, for they were only symptoms. I had to get back to the source: fear of judgment, fear of being criticized and condemned, fear of rejection.

I am confident I would never have discovered this had it not been for my participation in a Yokefellow group, which stimulated me to engage in a half-hour quiet time daily, and the tests I took.

The fear that such a group will become morbidly introspective is baseless, originating in psychological defensiveness. Such a fear is usually based on a fear of discovering things about ourselves which we do not want to face.

I recommend a sharing group by whatever name, one in which the participants are not encouraged to pray about symptoms, but to search for the basic cause of the symptoms.

To pray effectively one must be cleansed of the four fundamental barriers, which prevent the power of God from operating in your life. They are fear, hate, inferiority, and guilt. Only through diligent searching, with ruthless honesty, can these be dredged up.

Since we humans have powerful unconscious defense systems at work, most of us can profit from a suitable sharing group, with spiritual growth inventories, in order to discover the life-long barriers which limit our effectiveness, impair our relationships, and dim our vision of the Eternal God, who seeks constantly to pour out his blessings into our lives.

Simon Peter wrote two lovely letters to his fellow Christians. In one of them the rough old former fisherman momentarily becomes poetic and looks forward to the time when ". . . the day dawns and the morning star rises in your hearts." [9]

Until that day may the God of peace grant you the deepest desires of your heart!

Notes

Introduction
  1. Ps. 19:12.

Chapter 1: Success and Failure in Prayer
  1. 2 Cor. 12:9.
  2. Matt. 14:30.
  3. Matt. 9:29, KJV.
  4. Jer. 29:13.
  5. 1 John 3:21.
  6. See Mark 7:20–23; 12:28–31.
  7. 1 Cor. 3:21.
  8. Eph. 3:20.
  9. John 6:34.
  10. Ps. 37:4.

Chapter 2: Your Faith Can Make You Whole—Or Sick
  1. Acts 12:15–16, TEV.
  2. Eph. 3:20.
  3. Ps. 22:27.
  4. Rom. 8:28.
  5. Mark 9:23.

Chapter 3: Give Me Patience, Lord—Right Now!
  1. 1 Cor. 13:4.
  2. Gal. 2:11, KJV.
  3. John 7:16, Phillips.
  4. Ps. 46:10.
  5. Isa. 30:15.
  6. 2 Cor. 10:7–16.

Chapter 4: Formulas for Effective Prayer
  1. Gen. 4:9.
  2. Gal. 5:6.

Chapter 5: Steps in Practical Prayer
  1. Matt. 6:10–11.
  2. James 4:3.
  3. Jer. 29:13.
  4. Gal. 5:6.
  5. Luke 17:17.
  6. "Count Your Blessings," Johnson Oatman, Jr.
  7. Matt. 6:9–10.
  8. Ps. 46:10.
  9. Luke 12:34.
  10. Eph. 3:20.
  11. Gen. 18:14.
  12. Matt. 11:28.
  13. John 15:7.

Chapter 6: God Wills Wholeness of Body, Mind, and Circumstance

1. Andrew Weil, *The Natural Mind: A New Way of Looking at Drugs and the Higher Consciousness* (New York: Houghton, Mifflin, 1972), pp. 142–43.

2. Matt. 12:15.   3. Mark 6:5–6.

4. Luke 13:16.

5. See Arthur Janov, *The Primal Scream: Primal Therapy, the Cure for Neurosis* (New York: G. P. Putnam's Sons, 1970); and Arthur Janov, *The Primal Revolution* (New York: Simon & Schuster).

Chapter 7: Guilt, Forgiveness, and Prayer

1. John 8:11.   2. 1 John 3:21.

Chapter 8: The Fear of God Can Be the Beginning of Neurosis

1. Luke 12:48.   2. Micah 6:8.

3. John 14:9.   4. John 10:30.

5. See Matt. 6:24–33.   6. Matt. 22:36–39.

7. Matt. 5:43–48.   8. Luke 6:38.

9. Matt. 18:21, 22.

Chapter 9: Answered and Unanswered Prayer

1. Job 13:24.   2. Job 19:25.

3. Matt. 27:46.   4. 2 Cor. 12:9, NEB.

5. 2 Cor. 11:23–27; 12:1–4.

6. John 16:33, NEB.   7. Matt. 28:20.

8. William R. Parker and E. St. Johns, *Prayer Can Change Your Life* (New York: Prentice-Hall, 1957).

9. 2 Pet. 1:19.